NEW STUDIES IN BIBLICAL THEOLOGY 64

IMPOSSIBLE TO BE RESTORED?

'Marcus Mininger has written a truly new and paradigm changing interpretation of the warning passages in the Book of Hebrews. In particular, his treatment of Hebrews 6:1-6 provides a new and convincing lens through which to understand this difficult passage. His exegesis is careful and comprehensive, and ultimately persuasive. I commend this book to those interested in the topic of apostasy in general and especially the concept of "falling away" from the faith in Hebrews. The conclusions also have pastoral implications.'
Dr G. K. Beale, Professor of New Testament, Reformed Theological Seminary, Dallas, TX

'*Impossible to be Restored?* adds further lustre to the already fine series of New Studies in Biblical Theology. Like G. K. Chesterton's Father Brown (who solved crimes by "committing them" himself) Marcus Mininger suggests a solution to some of the puzzles in Hebrews by following the clues that lead us into the sitz im leben of its first hearers. By doing so he provides a coherent interpretation of its warning passages (notably Hebrews 6:4-6).

The result is a study that functions at several different levels. To the scholar it offers a careful and stimulating study that serves to loosen an exegetical knot with which theologians have struggled for centuries. To the hard-pressed theological student it gives an (always welcome!) crash course in recent scholarly work on Hebrews. And, not least, to pastors, preachers, and counsellors it provides biblical exposition that will inform their preaching and their ability to give a helpful reading of Scripture not least to troubled souls. All in all, *Impossible to be Restored?* is a gift to the church.'
Dr Sinclair B. Ferguson, Chancellor Professor of Systematic Theology, Reformed Theological Seminary

'Marcus Mininger carefully analyses Hebrews' warning about the impossibility of repentance for apostates (Hebrews 6:4). After thoroughly reviewing diverse scholarly opinions, he reformulates a traditional reading of Hebrews' situation. The epistle warns its addressees not to avoid persecution by reverting to Jewish practices, the "foundation" of faith (Hebrews 6:1). Reconciliation to Christ remains possible for serious sinners; retracing the initial path to him through the old covenant is not. A thoughtful exploration of pastoral implications concludes his treatment. Anyone interested in a central theological "crux" of Hebrews will welcome this research.'
Dr Harold W. Attridge, Sterling Professor of Divinity, Yale University

'I commend this book for setting forth what in my opinion is a definitive advance in understanding the apostasy passages in the book of Hebrews, with special focus on Hebrews 6:–16. It resolves by careful exegesis the difficulties

belonging to a most vexing and disputed passage. Moreover, it has practical implications for how theologians think about apostasy and how the church should deal with people who have abandoned the faith or are contemplating it. The book underlines vigorously the fact that Christ is the only way of salvation, thus also providing resources for answering the modern attempts to find an opening for salvation through other religions.'
Dr Vern S. Poythress, Distinguished Professor of New Testament, Biblical Interpretation, and Systematic Theology, Westminster Theological Seminary

'A person with a fresh perspective poses questions that have ceased to be asked. This fresh inquiry is what Mininger has brought to the study of Hebrews. The questions he poses are fresh, but not naïve. He has devoted years of scholarly investigation to find suitable answers for some of the most difficult sections of this powerful letter. Insightful, thorough, gracious and pastoral, *Impossible to Be Restored?* should become a necessary conversation partner for all those interested in the background, text and impact of the Epistle to the Hebrews.'
Dr Amy Peeler, Kenneth T. Wessner Professor of New Testament, Wheaton College

'Mininger's arguments are impressive. He well argues that the letter is addressed to those primarily influenced by Judaism, to which I agree. Although this is not an unusual conclusion, his argumentation for it, including a fair explanation of those who disagree, is excellent. Beyond this, Mininger's primary burden is to solve many of the difficulties with Hebrews 6:1–6. His solution is that the "impossible to restore again to repentance" text refers to the *impossibility to return to the Old Covenant for redemptive-historical reasons.* This conclusion needs to be considered seriously by the scholarly world, and more especially, the evangelical world. Although in the end, I disagree with Mininger on this, I am wholeheartedly in favour of this view being included as one of the standard views on Hebrews 6.'
Dr Robert J. Cara, Hugh and Sallie Reaves Professor of New Testament, Reformed Theological Seminary, Charlotte, NC

'Nothing in Hebrews has proven to be more perplexing, for some even confounding, nothing has resulted in a more wide-ranging and complex spectrum of views than the meaning of those passages that warn against the temptation to apostasy, especially in chapters 6 and 10. This volume makes an important and welcome contribution to this complicated debate. Future treatments of these passages are bound to benefit from considering the thesis – based on thorough research, carefully and clearly argued – that Mininger

advances. Beneficial too are the valuable insights he provides into the theology of Hebrews as a whole.'
Dr Richard B. Gaffin, Jr., Professor of Biblical and Systematic Theology, Emeritus, Westminster Theological Seminary

'Here is a carefully argued and clearly articulated approach to solving some of the stickier interpretative issues in Hebrews. Mininger offers fresh insights into Hebrews in light of its place in redemptive history, and helps us consider how this letter continues to speak to us today.'
Dr Brandon Crowe, Professor of New Testament, Westminster Theological Seminary

'Marcus Mininger has helpfully reconsidered the problem addressed in Hebrews and the author's way of dealing with it. He offers a careful critique of both traditional and revisionist positions, asking whether the audience of Hebrews was tempted to return to the *old covenant* rather than to "Judaism" as such. Eight traditional views of the warning passages are critiqued and Mininger proposes that a radical "situational change" from a new covenant position is what makes it impossible for some people to be restored to repentance. This book provides excellent resources for advancing our understanding of this critical issue.'
Dr David Peterson, Emeritus faculty member at Moore Theological College, Sydney

'In this thorough study of Hebrews' warning against apostasy, Marcus Mininger effectively exposes the shortcomings of existing interpretive approaches before offering a fresh and convincing reading that has been hiding in plain sight. His redemptive-historical interpretation, focusing on the impossibility of returning from the new covenant to the old covenant alone, aligns seamlessly with both the letter's theological argument and the broader biblical witness. Through careful exegesis and theological insight, Mininger not only illuminates this challenging text but also deepens our understanding of how Hebrews views the relationship between the covenants. Importantly, his objective covenantal reading helps relieve the subjective anxieties this passage often causes, showing that it warns not against an "unforgivable sin" that prevents a return to Christ, but against attempting to find refuge in the old covenant after having entered the new. This is biblical-theological scholarship at its finest—historically informed, exegetically rigorous, and theologically astute.'
Dr Camden Bucey, Executive Director and Fellow, Reformed Forum

NEW STUDIES IN BIBLICAL THEOLOGY 64

Series editors: D. A. Carson and Benjamin L. Gladd

IMPOSSIBLE TO BE RESTORED?

Temptation and Warning in the Epistle of Hebrews

Marcus A. Mininger

Published in Great Britain by APOLLOS (an imprint of Inter-Varsity Press)
SPCK Group, Studio 101, The Record Hall, 16–16A Baldwin's Gardens, London
EC1N 7RJ, England
Email: ivp@ivpbooks.com
Website: www.ivpbooks.com

Published in the USA by B&H Academic®, Brentwood, Tennessee

All Scripture quotations, including the Septuagint, are the author's own translations.

First published 2025

British Library Cataloguing-in-Publication Data
A catalogue record for this book is available from the British Library.

Apollos ISBN: 978–1–78974–579–5
eBook ISBN: 978–1–78974–580–1

Library of Congress Cataloging-in-Publication Data is on file at the Library of Congress, Washington, DC

B&H Academic ISBN 979–8–3845–3443–3
eBook ISBN 979–8–3845–3444–0

30 29 28 27 26 25 VP 1 2 3 4 5 6 7 8 9 10

Typeset by Fakenham Prepress Solutions, Fakenham, Norfolk NR21 8NL
Printed in the United States of America

Produced on paper from sustainable sources

Inter-Varsity Press publishes Christian books that are true to the Bible and that communicate the gospel, develop discipleship and strengthen the church for its mission in the world.

IVP originated within the Inter-Varsity Fellowship, now the Universities and Colleges Christian Fellowship, a student movement connecting Christian Unions in universities and colleges throughout Great Britain, and a member movement of the International Fellowship of Evangelical Students. Website: www.uccf.org.uk. That historic association is maintained, and all senior IVP staff and committee members subscribe to the UCCF Basis of Faith.

To Hans, Anastasia and Malena,
part of the next generation of Today.

May you remain steadfast in your confession,
assembling with confidence,
striving by faith in our unseen Saviour,
until we all enter the great Rest.

Contents

Tables

Series preface

New Studies in Biblical Theology is a series of monographs that address key issues in the discipline of biblical theology. Contributions to the series focus on one or more of three areas: (1) the nature and status of biblical theology, including its relations with other disciplines (e.g. historical theology, exegesis, systematic theology, historical criticism, narrative theology); (2) the articulation and exposition of the structure of thought of a particular biblical writer or corpus; and (3) the delineation of a biblical theme across all or part of the biblical corpora.

Above all, these monographs are creative attempts to help thinking Christians understand their Bibles better. The series aims simultaneously to instruct and to edify, to interact with the current literature and to point the way ahead. In God's universe, mind and heart should not be divorced: in this series we will try not to separate what God has joined together. While the notes interact with the best of scholarly literature, the text is uncluttered with untransliterated Greek and Hebrew, and tries to avoid too much technical jargon. The volumes are written within the framework of confessional evangelicalism, but there is always an attempt at thoughtful engagement with the sweep of the relevant literature.

Dr Mininger's *Impossible to be Restored?* takes another look at some of the most perplexing passages in Scripture. His insights are as insightful as they are theologically informed. We commend this volume to those wanting to take another look at the book of Hebrews and the believers' relationship to the Mosaic covenant.

D. A. Carson
Trinity Evangelical Divinity School

Benjamin L. Gladd
The Carson Center for Theological Renewal

Author's preface

This book had its earliest beginnings when I was asked to teach a seminary course on the biblical theology of the New Testament while still a graduate student. The course was designed to study some of the New Testament's major teachings about the unfolding of God's work of redemption through history. How does the New Testament describe the process by which God accomplished and is continuing to accomplish salvation through Christ, beginning in the past, continuing into the present and extending into the ultimate, eschatological future? Naturally, a course like that can easily spend a lot of time in Hebrews, since it is the New Testament text that reflects most directly and at greatest length on such topics. It is also fitting that content on such topics should now appear in a series titled New Studies in Biblical Theology.

While a teaching opportunity provided the occasion for this project's inception, the heart of the project has always been a strong desire to deal fairly with some particular passages of Scripture whose wording and apparent meaning are especially challenging. Interpreting Scripture is a complex process influenced by various factors. For example, as we study any given passage, we are influenced by doctrinal conclusions that we arrived at previously and by what we already think other Scripture texts say on related topics. If we believe that Scripture is normative for our lives today, we are also influenced by what we expect or hope any given passage does or does not say, since that has consequences for what we ourselves should believe or do. Factors such as these inevitably put pressure on us as we read, thereby predisposing us towards some interpretative conclusions and away from others. Yet while it is only natural to feel some of these pressures as we read, our deepest desire should still be to listen to what the text itself says and to understand it on its own terms.

However, though this goal is relatively simple in theory, it is actually quite challenging and soul-searching in practice. In the case of Hebrews, the most puzzling issue that confronted me early on in my study was how to understand the words in Hebrews 6:4–6 about the impossibility of some enlightened people being restored to repentance, as well as other similar warning statements throughout the letter. Inevitably, my pre-existing sense of what other passages in the New Testament teach on related topics came into play. This especially included other passages about falling away from faith and about unforgiven sins, but it also brought to mind certain scriptures that teach about the radical nature of forgiveness, for example in the lives of people such as Peter and Paul; about God's infallible preservation of his own to the end, so that nothing can separate them from his love; and about how Christ knows and will lose none of his sheep. Naturally, various biblical passages had instilled a general set of expectations in me regarding what I thought the warning texts in Hebrews were probably saying or not. Yet at the same time, these pre-existing expectations, while natural enough to have in one way or another, could easily impair my ability to listen to Hebrews on its own terms, from within its own world-view. This danger makes it all the more important to try to read the words of Hebrews in their original context, which is part of why this book also closely considers the situation of Hebrews' original audience and especially what temptation that audience was facing – a temptation to which the author's warnings were a carefully crafted response.

Though many factors inevitably influence our reading of Scripture, then, we should be guided and animated most of all by an honest and transparent desire not simply to prove that a passage means something we are comfortable with but to try to hear it in its own voice. What can the exact words on the page most fairly be understood to mean within their original setting? And when and where do past interpreters seem to be describing the details of a given passage in a way that genuinely illumines the text, rather than overlooking or sitting in tension with important aspects of it? Truly, these relatively simple questions present a bracing challenge. There are so many subtle ways in which we can all easily go wrong when seeking to answer them.

As the chapters below will describe, past interpretation of Hebrews does often seem neglectful of, or at odds with, some of the details found in the passages we are set to explore. When we observe such problems, they should challenge us to read and reread the passages in search of better clues to their meaning, as well as to read and reread ourselves to see what perspective we are lacking. What is it that we or others are overlooking or making wrong assumptions about or somehow misconstruing? What additional information or alternative angle can better illuminate the whole of a given text, making sense of all its details in a more natural way?

When seeking to answer those questions, careful reconsideration has led me to defend some old interpretations of certain topics and to offer a substantively new interpretation of others. But whether these interpretative results are deemed a success or not should not be decided on the basis of whether I or anyone else *likes* them or whether they fit within any given person's existing convictions or preferences. It should instead be decided in relation to the larger goal of the investigation itself: to make better sense of exactly what the author of Hebrews does and does not say in various key texts, and why.

Yet to say that we must continue seeking to hear Scripture on its own terms is definitely *not* to say that we should read it alone or in isolation from other interpreters. Far from it. If we are being at all responsible, we will always be standing on others' shoulders when we read and depending heavily on their interpretative efforts. And this is true both when we agree with what they have said and when we end up disagreeing. Either way, their efforts benefit us greatly, providing crucial insights and creating a rich context within which to observe, ask questions and find clues to what might be missing in our understanding.

With this in mind, I want to acknowledge some of the debt that I owe to others – individuals who gave me particular help throughout this project. Of course, a large amount of that debt is acknowledged in the footnotes found throughout the book, which reference the work of a broad stream of Hebrews scholars – something like a great cloud of witnesses – who have run the race before me and continue to help, inspire and challenge me.

Yet, in addition to this broad expression of gratitude, a special word of appreciation goes to Dr Amy Peeler, a colleague and friend. Amy gave generously of her time at several junctures to read some earlier and regrettably less clear versions of this book's content, and she graciously offered both ample encouragement and sage advice. In fact, it was she who suggested that I should treat, not just the warning in Hebrews, but also the question of what specific temptation the audience faced, since they are so interrelated. This wise suggestion and the rest of her input helped to make the present book much more substantive and well-rounded.

I am also thankful to Drs Eric Mason and Madison Pierce, co-chairs of SBL's Hebrews Session, who gave me the opportunity to read two different papers and to get helpful interaction from distinguished colleagues in that group. Dr Mason also went above and beyond by giving his time to dialogue in person – always with the utmost grace – and even sent substantive written comments afterwards, which helped me to see some particular areas of weakness and unclarity in my formulations at that time. Since Dr Mason and I do, in the end, hold substantively different positions regarding various topics treated in this book, his cordial engagement was all the more noteworthy and appreciated, a true example of broad-minded collegiality from an established and respected figure within the biblical studies guild.

While it is nice to have ideas for books to write, concrete opportunities to actually research and compose them can be difficult to find. I am grateful, then, to the Board of Trustees of Mid-America Reformed Seminary, in Dyer, Indiana, for a sabbatical in the autumn of 2018, which allowed me to investigate deeply into my topic and write significant parts of the book. I am also grateful to the seminary's board; its past president, Dr Cornel Venema; and the teaching staff in general, who always monitored my workload so that I could continue researching and writing even during non-sabbatical semesters. Dr Alan Strange, faculty colleague and now Interim President of Mid-America, took the time to read the text, interact with me and provide heartfelt encouragement about the project at several stages along the way. Students at Mid-America have also heard much of the content of this book at various stages of development over the last thirteen years in a course on the General Epistles and Revelation; their patience and helpful interaction are both greatly appreciated. For these and other reasons, I count it a distinct privilege to work at such an institution, where teaching and scholarship are valued and supported in sacrificial ways, including through the generous giving of faithful donors who value the seminary's mission.

Thanks are also due to Dr D. A. Carson, who graciously read and took interest in my manuscript, opening the door to its being published in this distinguished series. It has been a privilege for me to get to know Don in recent years. His kindness, frankness, rigorous thinking and love for Scripture are each such a wonderful example and source of encouragement. I am also grateful to Dr Ben Gladd and Thomas Creedy for their editorial contributions, which have been a great help and added significant value to the project. In addition, two students, Daniel Hofland and Joshua Savage, and a recent acquaintance, Chloe

Brittain, generously volunteered editorial and other feedback, which I appreciate.

Beyond all of this, I am most grateful to my friend, co-heir and fellow pilgrim, Chandra, who has been my *sine qua non* – at least humanly speaking – almost ever since I have known her. With her, I dedicate this book to our children, Hans, Anastasia and Malena, who are increasingly not just our children but our peers and friends. I pray that they will always know the joy that is set before them in Christ and so have great confidence and endurance, through thick and thin, as we make a pilgrimage together towards a future life in a far greater City – that wonderfully satisfying, though as-yet-unseen dwelling place, whose architect, builder and source of glory is none other than our great God himself.

Abbreviations

Journals, lexica, etc.

AB	Anchor Bible
ANTC	Abingdon New Testament Commentaries
BECNT	Baker Exegetical Commentary on the New Testament
BSac	*Bibliotheca Sacra*
BZNW	Beihefte zur Zeitschrift für die neutestamentliche Wissenschaft
CBQ	*Catholic Biblical Quarterly*
CBQMS	Catholic Biblical Quarterly Monograph Series
CBR	*Currents in Biblical Research*
CCSS	Catholic Commentary on Sacred Scripture
CTJ	*Calvin Theological Journal*
EBib	Evangelical Biblical Theology Commentary
FRLANT	Forschungen zur Religion und Literatur des Alten und Neuen Testaments
HTR	*Harvard Theological Review*
IVPNTC	IVP New Testament Commentary
JSNTSup	Journal for the Study of the New Testament Supplement Series
KEK	Kritisch-exegetischer Kommentar über das Neue Testament
LNTS	Library of New Testament Studies
LXX	Septuagint
MThZ	*Münchener Theologische Zeitschrift*
NA-27	Nestle-Aland Novum Testamentum Graece, 27th edn
NA-28	Nestle-Aland Novum Testamentum Graece, 28th edn
NICNT	New International Commentary on the New Testament
NIDNTTE	*New International Dictionary of New Testament Theology and Exegesis*, ed. M. Silva, 2nd edn, 5 vols., Grand Rapids: Zondervan, 2014
NIGTC	New International Greek Testament Commentary

NovT	*Novum Testamentum*
NovTSup	Novum Testamentum Supplements
NSBT	New Studies in Biblical Theology
NT	New Testament
NTL	New Testament Library
NTS	*New Testament Studies*
OT	Old Testament
P[46]	Papyrus 46 (*P. Chester Beatty II*)
PNTC	Pillar New Testament Commentary
SBL	Society of Biblical Literature
SCDS	Studies in Christian Doctrine and Scripture
SNTSMS	Society for New Testament Studies Monograph Series
SP	Sacra Pagina
TDNT	*Theological Dictionary of the New Testament*, ed. G. Kittel and G. Friedrich, tr. G. W. Bromiley, 10 vols., Grand Rapids: Eerdmans, 1964–76
TNTC	Tyndale New Testament Commentaries
TrinJ	*Trinity Journal*
UBS-5	United Bible Societies Greek New Testament, 5th edn
WBC	Word Biblical Commentary
WTJ	*Westminster Theological Journal*
ZECNT	Zondervan Exegetical Commentary on the New Testament

Ancient texts

Epictetus	
Diss.	*Dissertationes*
Josephus	
Ag. Ap.	*Against Apion*
Ant.	*Jewish Antiquities*
J.W.	*Jewish War*
Philo	
Agriculture	*On Agriculture*
Alleg. Interp.	*Allegorical Interpretation*
Cherubim	*On the Cherubim*
Contempl. Life	*On the Contemplative Life*
Creation	*On the Creation of the World*
Dreams	*On Dreams*
Drunkenness	*On Drunkenness*

Embassy	*On the Embassy to Gaius*
Giants	*On Giants*
Good Person	*That Every Good Person Is Free*
Heir	*Who Is the Heir?*
Migration	*On the Migration of Abraham*
Moses	*On the Life of Moses*
Names	*On the Change of Names*
Prelim. Studies	*On the Preliminary Studies*
Rewards	*On Rewards and Punishments*
Sacrifices	*On the Sacrifices of Cain and Abel*
Virtues	*On the Virtues*

1

Introduction: the mystery of Hebrews and the search for context

More than perhaps any other document in the New Testament, the epistle of Hebrews has proven itself to be quite a puzzle for modern interpreters. Harold Attridge calls Hebrews the 'most enigmatic' text of first-century Christianity, noting how the circumstances surrounding its composition are 'mysterious'.[1] Similarly, Craig Koester has said, 'By the end of the twentieth century . . . Hebrews came to be called the riddle of the New Testament.'[2] As commentators often acknowledge, the reasons for such widespread puzzlement have much to do with two related factors. The first concerns what it is that modern scholars believe is important to know about a text in order to interpret it properly. The second concerns what the text of Hebrews does and does not actually say about itself and its context. By virtue of their own instincts and training, modern scholars focus on certain kinds of details about the author, audience, date and larger historical context of any document, in order to try to understand the document well. Yet for its part, Hebrews remains quite taciturn about those exact topics. As a result, a general state of puzzlement pervades recent scholarship on Hebrews and provides part of the reason for the present study, which will seek to shed new light on some aspects of this enigmatic text.

The pages below will therefore offer some new explorations into the study of Hebrews, seeking to bring some details about it to light that have gone overlooked in the past but are particularly important for

[1] Attridge 1989: 1.

[2] Koester 2001: 42. See similar statements in Hughes 1977: 1; Bruce 1990: 3; Lane 1991: xlvii; L. T. Johnson 2006: 1; Thompson 2008: 3.

understanding its context and key aspects of its message. While there are many topics that are, and likely always will remain, mysterious about the original context of Hebrews, the exegesis below will try to show that there are certain topics that the text of Hebrews *does* make clearer than scholars have often thought, especially regarding the nature of the principal temptation that Hebrews addresses and the nature of the warning it sounds in response to that temptation. Both of these topics are crucial for interpreting this particular document, so understanding them better will also shed significant light on the book as a whole. In what follows, then, we will especially seek to answer three big questions. What exact temptation especially faces the audience of Hebrews at the time the author writes to them? What exactly is his principal warning to them in response to that temptation? And how does all of that help us to better understand this theologically robust and pastorally fervent document?

What remains unknown about Hebrews' context

When approaching any biblical text, modern interpreters are typically eager to identify certain features of its historical context, as the introduction to any scholarly commentary shows. Customarily, this desire for historical contextualization focuses on topics such as who the author is, who the audience is, where and when both lived, when the document was written, what other historically significant factors existed at or around that time, and what pressures both author and audience were experiencing and responding to in their environment. In addition, recent interpretative trends have also led towards a particularly heightened concern for defining context with regard to more specific topics about the author, audience and those around them, such as their ethnicity, sex, wealth or poverty, and other socio-economic factors. Is a given author or audience Jewish, Gentile or mixed; male or female; rich, poor or mixed; socially influential, marginal or mixed; and so forth? To be sure, knowledge about all these topics is very helpful for interpretation whenever it is available. In principle, the more we know about the specific historical context within which a text arose, the better we should be able to understand both the meaning of its words and the rhetorical impact those words were meant to have on its original recipients.[3] After all, interpreting a text without attention to historical context can allow its words to be more easily twisted by a reader's own assumptions or preferences, to the point where it can seem to mean something that it originally did not. As the saying goes, a text without a context becomes a pretext, that is, an occasion for us to read our own preferred meanings *into* it. At base, then, the impulse to reconstruct the original historical context is quite helpful and, to some extent, even necessary for disciplined reading, especially when it comes to ancient texts that arose in time periods and circumstances that are often quite foreign to our own. Reconstructing the original context of a document should help us to read it more closely and accurately.

Yet, while historical reconstruction is inherently valuable, it is equally true that figuring out the original context of the epistle of Hebrews is notoriously difficult, and much of the reason for that originates in Hebrews itself: what it does or does not say within its own pages. In short, the author to the Hebrews chooses to say relatively little about himself or his audience, and what he does say often does not address the kinds of topics that modern interpreters would naturally be most interested to know for the sake of historical reconstruction. For example, though Hebrews bears some of the marks of an epistle at its *conclusion*, such as a request for prayer (13:18), expression of a desire to visit the audience (13:19), news about shared associates (13:23), greetings (13:24) and blessings (13:20–21, 25), it does not include a typical letter-*opening*,[4] and, partly because of this, the author does not directly identify either himself or his audience anywhere in the document.

Beyond not identifying himself overtly, though, the author of Hebrews does not provide much information of another kind that would help to

[3] On a related note, D. A. Carson and Douglas J. Moo correctly note that explanations of the purpose of Hebrews, which are quite crucial to understanding the letter as a whole, always rely significantly on some understanding of the situation of the original audience (see Carson and Moo 2005: 609). It is precisely for this reason that select elements of the original audience's situation related to the temptation they face will be studied carefully below.

[4] The genre of Hebrews has been heavily debated, particularly regarding the extent to which it should be classified as an epistle or as a homily. While scholars generally recognize that Hebrews is something of a hybrid between the two, some more strongly emphasize the former genre-identification, such as Lindars 1991: 7; Ellingworth 1993: 62. But most scholars put greater emphasis on its sermonic qualities; see Attridge 1989: 14; Lane 1991: xlvii; Koester 2001: 80–81; L. T. Johnson 2006: 33; Mitchell 2007: 17; Witherington 2007: 20; Thompson 2008: 13; Hooker 2009: 189; Peeler 2014: 1 n. 1; D. E. Johnson 2018: 22. Given the document's hybrid characteristics, I will refer to it both as a letter and as a sermon, though the latter is surely more descriptive regarding its purposes and its manner of accomplishing them, as Attridge notes.

identify him. Unlike the apostle Paul, for example, who tends to be very forward about his own situation and experiences when he writes, the author of Hebrews does not speak frequently about himself, and so there is not much to go on when trying to identify him. We can certainly deduce various things about him, of course, such as that he is quite educated and writes in a noticeably elegant style of Greek, especially compared to other early Christian authors.[5] His argument also makes very heavy use of the Old Testament Scriptures in Greek translation (the so-called Septuagint) as well as various terms and phrases that are familiar from Greek philosophy, including Middle Platonism.[6] For these and other reasons, supposing (as many do) that someone such as Apollos may have written Hebrews remains an attractive idea, since Apollos was a rhetorically gifted Jew, was educated in the Scriptures, and hailed from Alexandria (Acts 18:24) where Greek philosophies including Platonism were clearly being used to help interpret Scripture by other first-century authors such as Philo of Alexandria. In the end, though, the suggestion that Apollos wrote Hebrews remains entirely speculative, and the author's identity simply remains unknown, as is widely acknowledged in scholarship today. One of the enduring puzzles about Hebrews, then, concerns who wrote it, a basic detail about the document that we simply remain ignorant of, largely because the author did not choose to incorporate many details about himself into his own writing.

Of course, it is apparent from Hebrews that the original audience knew who the author was anyway, since he says he wants to visit them again and asks for their prayers towards that end (13:18–19). Nevertheless, while the original audience gets the benefit of knowing who the author is, the fact that he did not feel the need to incorporate or comment on almost anything about himself in his writing is something which we, as modern readers, should take note of as an indication of what he did and did not find important to focus on as he communicated his desired message. Evidently, this author's emphasis simply lies elsewhere.

---

[5] Many note that the Greek in Hebrews is the best Greek of any in the New Testament. See Lane 1991: xlix; Lindars 1991: 2; Witherington 2007: 19; Thompson 2008: 6; Gray and Peeler 2020: 4.

[6] For descriptions of the thought-background of the author, including his creative appropriation of certain Platonic categories, see Barrett 1964: 363–393; Koester 2001: 98–100; L. T. Johnson 2006: 7, 17–21; Thompson 2008: 23–26; 2011.

Similar observations can also be made about identifying who the audience of Hebrews was. Interestingly, the author actually says more to his audience about them than about himself, such as when he narrates back to them some of their own past experiences of joy in the midst of persecution after they had become Christians (10:32–34), or what had happened when they first heard and believed the Christian message from others who had been eyewitnesses of Jesus' own earthly ministry (2:3–4). In the latter of these descriptions, unlike the former, most scholars believe the author does include himself, since he describes how the message first declared by Christ was then 'attested to *us* by those who heard' (2:3).[7] Still, the historical detail that the author provides about either himself or his audience remains quite sparse, at least when it comes to topics that modern interpreters would especially prioritize for interpretation. In fact, when the author does describe his audience's situation, he tends to prioritize descriptions that locate them in reference to God's own supernatural, revelatory activity, rather than in more ordinary historical terms. For example, he identifies the time period in which they live as 'the last of these days' when God has spoken through his Son, in contrast to the time 'long ago' when he spoke through prophets (1:1–2a). He also says that they heard about Jesus from those who had been eyewitnesses of Jesus' ministry (2:3–4) and through this were 'enlightened' about the work of Christ as high priest in the period of God's having established a new covenant with his people (10:32 and surrounding context). Such descriptions do provide an understanding of the time period when the audience lived, but not with much specificity. It does, however, seem clear from the letter that either the author or (more likely) the audience lived in Italy, since the conclusion of the letter communicates greetings from those who are 'from Italy' (13:24).[8] In addition, most scholars believe that the author and audience have some connection to the Pauline circle of associates, not least because of the author's expressed desire in 13:23 to travel with Timothy,

[7] Taking 2:3–4 as a description of both the author's and the audience's experience is almost universal among recent scholars, over against Eisenbaum 2005b: 227.

[8] Unlike older views that often placed the audience in Palestine, recent commentators tend to see 13:24 as a reference to where the audience is (rather than where the author is). Curiously, they also tend to go beyond what the author actually says in 13:24 by locating the audience specifically in Rome (not just Italy). Mitchell (2007: 7) notes that Rome is today's consensus. See also Attridge 1989: 10; Lane 1991: lviii; Ellingworth 1993: 29; Koester 2001: 49; Schenck 2007: 193; Witherington 2007: 19; Thomas 2008: 115; Schreiner 2020: 8–9; Cara 2024: 9. For helpful cautionary statements against being so specific, see Lindars 1991: 17; Thompson 2008: 7.

who is generally believed to be the same Timothy with whom Paul also travelled at times (see e.g. Acts 16:3; Phil. 1:1; 1 Thess. 1:1).[9] But beyond this, the identity and situation of the audience still remain fairly opaque to us, leaving a lot to be desired with respect to detail.

In addition, questions about the ethnicity of the audience, whether Jewish, Gentile or mixed, remain even more uncertain and have become a topic of considerable scholarly debate. The traditional view that the audience was composed of Jewish Christians remains popular today,[10] and this view would fit well with an ancient tradition that designated the letter as being written 'To the Hebrews'.[11] However, this viewpoint has been heavily contested in recent times, as will be discussed further below.[12] More importantly, arguments for either a Jewish or a Gentile audience tend to rely much more on inference than on anything the letter directly states, thereby not only leaving uncertainty about the correct conclusion but also raising questions regarding the extent to which the audience's ethnicity is especially *relevant* to the author's own concerns in this communication. In fact, because Hebrews does not even make mention of the terms 'Jew' or 'Gentile', some have wondered whether a decision about the ethnic make-up of the audience is really possible or even interpretatively very significant. As Patrick Gray and Amy Peeler note: 'based simply on the information found in the letter, it might be difficult to distinguish a Jewish audience from an audience of Gentile God-fearers who had been socialized and instructed in a Hellenistic synagogue.'[13] As so often happens in Hebrews interpretation, then, we may approach the text assuming that certain categories are important, such as 'Jew' and 'Gentile', but find that something else is mainly on the author's mind instead. This again

---

[9] Kenneth Schenck (2019: 8) notes that most scholars lean towards saying that the Timothy mentioned in Hebrews is in fact Paul's companion.

[10] Marshall 1975: 137; Hughes 1977: 11; Bruce 1990: 5–7; Lane 1991: cxxxv; Lindars 1991: 4; Witherington 2007: 210; Hays 2009: 165; Hooker 2009: 210; Stedman 2009: 11; Healy 2016: 20; D. E. Johnson 2018: 22; Schreiner 2020: 7; Cara 2024: 9.

[11] Witherington (2009: 19) notes that the designation 'To the Hebrews' is first known to occur in the late second century with Pantaenus, Clement of Alexandria and Tertullian, and Gray and Peeler (2020: 5) note that the first manuscript to designate Hebrews this way is P^{46} around the same time.

[12] Those affirming a predominantly Gentile audience include Schenck 2007: 42, 193–194; 2019: 18–19; Mitchell 2011: 254–255. Others argue for the audience likely being mixed, e.g. Ellingworth 1993: 25–26; deSilva 2000: 6–7; Grindheim 2023: 28–29.

[13] Gray and Peeler 2020: 6. Similarly, Koester (2001: 47–48) states: 'A simple distinction between Jewish and Gentile Christians does not help the interpretation of Hebrews.' See also Attridge 1989: 12; Eisenbaum 2005b: 233–234; L. T. Johnson 2006: 39.

requires us to seek to put aside assumptions and instead become attuned to someone else's world of thought in order to sympathetically appreciate and make good sense of what he wrote.

One other detail about Hebrews that remains uncertain concerns the date when the document was written. Certainly, the letter does include some temporal markers of a general kind, mentioned above, such as that the audience heard the Christian message of salvation from people who had been eyewitnesses of Jesus' own life and that they had been persecuted after they first made their Christian profession. But these details do not help to narrow things down significantly. To be sure, many have argued that the letter must have been written before Rome destroyed the Jewish temple in Jerusalem in AD 70, since the author never mentions the temple's destruction throughout the course of an otherwise lengthy argument about the superiority of Christ's priestly ministry to that of the old-covenant Levitical system, and he also speaks about the ministry of Levitical priests using present-tense verbs (e.g. Heb. 8:4, 13; 9:8–10; 13:10).[14] However, as plausible as a pre-70 date may be, the author's use of verb tenses cannot be decisive in itself, given the flexibility of present-tense verbs in Greek and the fact that other ancient authors continued to speak of the temple in the present tense even after it had been destroyed.[15] So, while plausible arguments can be made for various conclusions, certainty about the date of Hebrews remains elusive,[16] as is the case with so many other details about its original context.

In the final analysis, then, the historical context of Hebrews remains a mystery in many ways, including questions about its author, audience, location and date of composition. And the biggest reason for this has to do with Hebrews' own reticence to say much about such topics. As Pamela Eisenbaum notes, Hebrews is generally 'lacking in information related to questions of who, what, where, when, etc',[17] at least in the ways that modern interpreters tend to want to define such things.

---

[14] Those arguing for a pre-70 date include Hughes 1977: 31; Bruce 1990: 20–22; Lane 1991: lxvi, 64–68; Lindars 1991: 20–21; Ellingworth 1993: 33; deSilva 2000: 20; L. T. Johnson 2006: 40; Witherington 2007: 27; Healy 2016: 22; Gray and Peeler 2020: 9–10; Schreiner 2020: 6.

[15] See e.g. Josephus, *Ag. Ap.* 2.77; *1 Clement* 40:4–5; *Epistle to Diognetus* 3:1–5; also comments by Attridge 1989: 8; Koester 2001: 77; Eisenbaum 2005b: 225.

[16] Accordingly, Attridge (1989: 9) gives only a date range of AD 60–100 and Koester (2001: 50) of AD 60–90. Thompson (2008: 7) says that the date is unknown and not very important.

[17] Eisenbaum 2005b: 231.

Manufacturing greater certainty: speculative reconstruction

Given these factors, scholars often pause to reflect on the large amount that still remains unknown about Hebrews as well as the effect that this has on interpretation. According to Eisenbaum:

> The so-called 'Epistle to the Hebrews' is almost certainly the most mysterious text to have been preserved in the NT canon. The author's identity, the provenance, the addressees, and the date and occasion for writing are all widely disputed . . . Indeed, many scholars, myself included, have expressed resignation about ever possessing knowledge about Hebrews' chronological, geographical, and social situation, unless, perhaps, some miraculous new evidence appears . . . Although scholarly reconstructions of the social situation of Hebrews abound, there is virtually no specific information about the social context given in the text itself.[18]

Similarly, but with a more positive spin, William Lane says:

> Hebrews is a delight for the person who enjoys puzzles. Its form is unusual, its setting in life is uncertain, and its argument is unfamiliar. It invites engagement in the task of defining the undefined. Undefined are the identity of the writer, his conceptual background, the character and location of the community addressed, the circumstances and date of composition, the setting in life, the nature of the crisis to which the document is a response, the literary genre, and the purpose and plan of the work. Although these undefined issues continue to be addressed and debated vigorously, no real consensus has been reached.[19]

In fact, various scholars have whimsically compared the epistle of Hebrews to the ancient figure Melchizedek, whom Hebrews itself says was 'without father or mother or genealogy, having neither beginning of days nor end of life' (7:3).[20]

---

[18] Ibid. 213, 217.

[19] Lane 1991: xlvii.

[20] E.g. Koester 2001: 58; Witherington 2007: 17, citing L. T. Johnson 1999: 457; Hooker 2009: 189.

Yet, as common as it is for scholars to catalogue and comment on all the historical unknowns about Hebrews, the tension that most of them feel over this state of affairs remains quite palpable. After all, the reconstruction of historical context is a big part of what scholarship has characteristically relied upon to shed light on texts and to vindicate one interpretation over another. In this regard, Luke Timothy Johnson puts his finger on a significant pain-point for scholars studying Hebrews when he observes:

> In short, Hebrews challenges the capacity of the historical-critical approach to do what it does best. It reminds us of how little we really know about the history of earliest Christianity outside the framework established by the Acts of the Apostles and the letters of Paul.[21]

Not surprisingly, then, given the nature of this interpretative tension, it is almost as common to see scholars catalogue what remains unknown about Hebrews as it is to see them go on subsequently, through great effort, to fill the apparent gaps in our knowledge with significant amounts of conjecture in the name of greater interpretative clarity. For example, Philip Hughes reasoned as follows:

> What was the occasion that called forth this document? Because of the silence of the epistle itself and the absence of any external information or tradition which might provide a solution to this question, *the only alternative* to an incurious agnosticism is to attempt *to construct a conjectural answer*.[22]

Similarly, after describing Hebrews as a puzzle (quoted above), Lane goes on to say: 'As long as there are texts, there will be the challenge of reconstructing history from them, and historical methodology is *the only rational means* by which this can be done.'[23] Then he goes on to construct one of the most detailed hypotheses on record of Hebrews' exact context, using speculative reconstruction that seeks to infer specific information about the situation of the audience even from very small and seemingly

---

[21] L. T. Johnson 2006: 1.

[22] Hughes 1977: 10; emphasis added.

[23] Lane 1991: xlvii; emphasis added.

nondescript details in the text such as the fact that the author exhorts them to maintain the sanctity of marriage (13:4) or to beware of greed (13:5–6).[24] To similar effect, Eisenbaum, after describing Hebrews as mysterious and acknowledging that it says little about its social context (cited above), offers a warning against letting an 'abstract, often unhistorical . . . conception' of the text guide interpretation, and so turns to detailed analysis of 'the most concrete contextual information we possess about Hebrews', namely 'its genre, its affinity to or dissimilarity with other texts, and its textual history'.[25] Yet, as thought-provoking as Eisenbaum's consideration of such topics is, it nevertheless constitutes an attempt to make other topics that are *also* heavily debated and obscure, such as the later textual and reception history of Hebrews, provide clarity about the document in areas where Hebrews itself remains silent. In this way, Eisenbaum's method exemplifies the predicament that modern scholars often feel themselves to be in regarding Hebrews, and the speculative means they often resort to in order to achieve the kind of clarity about the letter's context that they instinctively believe is necessary for good interpretation.[26] In the end, though, many details about Hebrews remain shrouded in a considerable degree of mystery.

A helpful alternative: reconstructing Hebrews' thought-world from within

The challenge that Hebrews presents to modern interpretative assumptions, while real, need not simply function as a 'problem' to bemoan or to circumvent through reconstructive speculation. It should also be seen as *an opportunity* for contemporary readers to slow down, question our own assumptions of what is crucial to defining the context of a document, and seek to pay even more careful attention to this curiously reticent ancient text, whose perspective on context is often quite different from our own. As Marie Isaacs notes: 'Hebrews is indeed strange to the modern reader. It represents a conceptual world which is quite foreign to us'.[27] Yet this

[24] Ibid. liii.

[25] Eisenbaum 2005b: 217.

[26] See also the effort made by Iutisone Salevao (2002: 122) to provide the 'high level of specificity' in social reconstruction that is 'necessary for interpretation', despite acknowledging the lack of firm data for doing so.

[27] Isaacs 1992: 11.

state of affairs, according to which Hebrews inhabits and thinks within a different conceptual world from ours, need not be cause for lament. To the contrary, the 'mystery of Hebrews', as it has been described, offers an interpretative crucible, challenging us to put aside some of our pre-existing expectations about what kinds of textual knowledge make for good interpretation. Perhaps we can instead learn to listen and observe what Hebrews itself decides to mention about its context and what categories it uses when locating and characterizing itself, its audience and the circumstances that prompted its author to write in just the way he did. To be sure, Hebrews often places importance on very different things from those we would naturally focus on in our day, and works within a very different matrix of thought from our own. Just as surely, though, observing Hebrews' internal world of thought can help us to understand the document (and perhaps even ourselves) better.

In contrast to the general trend of speculative historical reconstruction, then, some scholars have advocated for greater restraint in interpretation, avoiding speculation on topics where detailed information is just not available.[28] Moreover, this interpretative restraint is often paired with advocacy for a greater focus on reconstructing the narrative thought-world of Hebrews from within its own pages. To this end, Kenneth Schenck notes how the history of Hebrews interpretation is often full of 'reckless guesses and unprovable hypotheses' about the author or background situation, and he therefore concludes: 'The only legitimate place to start interpreting Hebrews is with what the text of Hebrews itself tells us. Studies that begin by deciding on a highly specific author, audience, or situation are bound to lead us astray.'[29] Accordingly, Schenck has sought to articulate a more textually focused, narratival approach to interpreting Hebrews that gives prominence to Hebrews' own categories of thought, such as the spatial and temporal contrasts that are inherent to the author's expression of his own world-view.[30] While Schenck himself does end up drawing conclusions that may at times seem overly specific or misguided, as will be touched upon later, nevertheless the efforts that he and others

[28] See especially the sober historical assessments and desire not to over-conclude in the face of limited evidence often helpfully expressed in the commentaries of Attridge (1989), deSilva (2000), Koester (2001) and L. T. Johnson (2006).

[29] Schenck 2003: 1.

[30] See esp. Schenck 2007: 10–22; 2011: 171–188. For some similar emphases, see Thompson 2008: 21–26.

have made to emphasize the knowns of what the text *does* say over the unknowns of speculative reconstruction are quite salutary.

In addition, while seeking to stay disciplined by the text, Schenck points in a helpful direction regarding some topics that we can know more about concerning Hebrews' original context. Having acknowledged the shortcomings of much historical reconstruction, he nevertheless goes on to note that 'Hebrews does give us some general hints about its original situation'.[31] For example, building off Lloyd Bitzer and D. F. Watson, Schenck identifies and explores the helpful concept of the 'exigence' of Hebrews, that is, the way the author's and audience's situation involved 'an imperfection marked by urgency . . . a defect, an obstacle, something waiting to be done'.[32] In other words, Schenck believes that Hebrews gives important clues about why the author felt it was *necessary* to write Hebrews – why just this sort of document seemed necessary to pen for this particular audience when the author wrote. In particular, Schenck's analysis leads to a crucial question: what principal *problem* is Hebrews designed to address – a problem which then calls forth the particular kind of work that the author has in fact composed to address it? Or, put differently, whatever the larger *historical* situation of Hebrews may be, what can at least be said about the *rhetorical* situation of the letter, within which a perceived *problem* of some kind existed to which Hebrews was the ostensible *solution*?[33]

On reflection, the direction that Schenck has sketched out seems quite useful, both for remaining agnostic about many aspects of the historical context of Hebrews that simply evade clear definition and for defining the basic *problem* that Hebrews seeks to address and its core *response* to that problem. Particularly given the sermon-like qualities of Hebrews, which is a self-styled 'word of exhortation' (13:22; cf. Acts 13:15) that oscillates frequently between biblical exposition and strong exhortation directed to the audience,[34] it makes sense that something of the *burden* of such a document – the core concern to which it speaks and its chief message

[31] Schenck 2003: 1–2.

[32] Schenck 2007: 24.

[33] Ibid. 24–25.

[34] For influential discussions of the genre of Hebrews and its sermonic traits, see esp. Thyen 1955; Wills 1984; Attridge 1990; Gelardini 2005. See also the synthetic reflections on the topic in Lane 1991: lxix–lxxv. For thought-provoking reflections on Hebrews as an example of apostolic preaching and its possible use as a paradigm for preaching today, see D. E. Johnson 2007.

in relation to that concern – would be reflected clearly both in what the author says and in how he says it.

Unlike the situation, then, with many of the questions that scholars have focused upon, we will see that Hebrews actually has a significant amount to say that helps to define the principal temptation addressed and the repeated warning issued within its pages. Yet to see how this is so requires listening carefully to Hebrews' own discourse in a way that scholars sometimes have not done in the past. In this way, the project we embark upon presents a focused opportunity to hear the letter of Hebrews afresh. At the same time, it also provides an opportunity for us to reflect on and critique our own assumptions in order to decentre the exegetically unhelpful ones and so stay closer to and be more perceptive about the very text we want to understand.

The focus of this book: defining the main temptation and warning in Hebrews

Against the background of these tensions experienced in past Hebrews scholarship, the present study will make some new interpretative forays into the text of Hebrews, and in so doing it will suggest that, when we focus our attention on Hebrews' internal thought-world and seek to discern its own categories of thought, two crucial areas of the rhetorical situation of the document become clear. Despite many things that remain mysterious about it, Hebrews does offer important evidence to identify the key *temptation* that its audience faced when the author wrote and the key *warning* that the author articulated in response. More specifically, our investigation of the first topic will revolve around the question of whether the audience of Hebrews was tempted to return to Judaism or not. Traditionally, most scholars have thought that they were. But recently, an increasing number of scholars have not only challenged this notion but also called into question the interpretative biases that they believe underlie it – a development which calls for close re-examination of the topic. By comparison, our investigation of the second topic will focus especially on whether or not the author warns the audience that falling away from their Christian confession, or apostatizing, is something that has permanent results – something after which it becomes impossible to repent, be forgiven, and be restored to Christian fellowship and salvation. In this regard, readers of Hebrews have especially puzzled over the meaning of several of the letter's strongly worded warning passages. Perhaps most notably, what exactly does the stark language in Hebrews 6:4–6 really mean – that it is impossible for those who have fallen away from Christ to be restored to repentance? Does this articulate a kind of 'one and done' approach to the subject of apostasy, in which at least some who renounce Christianity can never turn from their error and be restored again to right standing with God? And if it does not mean that, what can the author's strongly worded statements be fairly understood to mean instead?

Before we embark on answering these key questions, though, a cautionary note is in order, to avoid the appearance of reductionism. Any document the size of Hebrews is no doubt quite complex, can be analysed at numerous different levels, probably has multiple problems that it addresses, and no doubt has many things that it says and seeks to accomplish. In what follows, then, we will not pretend that this study aims to be exhaustive. To the contrary, it will start out with a fairly narrow focus on some key texts – most notably Hebrews 6:1–6, but also other passages that include warnings such as 2:1–4; 3:7 – 4:13; 10:19–39; and 12:15–17 – before it then broadens out in its later chapters to make larger and more synthetic observations about Hebrews as a whole. As a result, this study will only touch on certain themes within Hebrews. But those themes will nevertheless open up a helpful perspective on the letter as a whole and on some of its distinctive ways of speaking that enable it to make a unique contribution to the content of the New Testament and to Christian thinking more generally.

Finally, no study of Scripture takes place in a vacuum. We are all part of a larger conversation about Scripture that helps to shape our own interpretation. Before advancing a constructive argument about Hebrews, then, it is quite important to look more closely at past scholarship itself, especially related to how each of the two main questions above has been answered before. Chapters 2 and 3 of this book will therefore look in turn at past scholarship on the temptation and the warning in Hebrews. This will allow us to understand the specific kinds of observations that scholars have used when formulating their own answers to our questions, where their chief interpretative assumptions and conclusions have been helpful, and where it is that new categories and solutions seem to be needed. It will also help to provide some parameters within which to re-examine crucial parts of Hebrews in chapters 4–7. In turn, all of this will lead to a closer reconsideration, in chapter 8, of some of Hebrews' deeper structures of thought, especially regarding the old and new covenants, and then to synthetic reflections on the pastoral relevance of Hebrews, both within its original context and, by extension, within our own context today, in chapter 9. Together, these steps should provide a detailed yet rewarding exegetical exploration.

2

Recent questions about the temptation: returning to Judaism or not?

When it comes to defining the main problem that the audience of Hebrews is facing when the author writes to them, some broad outlines of their situation are readily apparent. The author describes the audience's early history in a few places, including how they had originally heard the Christian message of salvation from eyewitnesses who had previously heard Jesus himself preach (2:3) and how they had received this message with remarkable confidence and joy even in the midst of the suffering and persecution that followed (10:32–35). Since that time, though, the audience's original zeal and conviction had clearly begun to wane. By the time the author writes, the audience should have been quite mature in the faith and able to teach others (5:12), but they are instead characterized by lack of attention or receptiveness to Christian teaching (being dull of hearing [5:11]), they may be fearful (10:32–36, 39), and they are likely growing weary (12:3, 5), so that the author must exhort them quite strongly not to give up their Christian profession but to continue forward in the confidence they had had before (3:14; 10:22, 35).

Yet while such a broad description of the audience's situation seems clear enough from Hebrews, a more specific question also arises: what particular temptation are they facing that would potentially draw them away from a Christian profession? Can the nature of the temptation be defined more closely?

The traditional paradigm

Until recently, scholars of Hebrews have generally thought that the answer to the above question was clear, that the principal temptation which Hebrews addresses is an inclination on the part of the audience to retreat from their Christian profession and find shelter instead in non-Christian Judaism.[1] While specific constructions of this general viewpoint have differed by degree, scholars have often thought that the audience was ethnically Jewish and that the temptation they faced was one of returning to a pre-Christian life in the synagogue and so to a form of Judaism that they had once experienced, prior to their hearing about and believing in Jesus as the Christ. As Barnabas Lindars summarizes:

> The traditional view is that Hebrews is written to a group of Jewish converts who are in danger of relapsing into Judaism . . . The aim of the letter is to persuade them to remain in the church with renewed confidence in the Christian confession of faith.[2]

Those espousing such a view generally believe that this understanding of the audience's situation helps to make sense of a variety of features of the letter. For example, the use of extensive and subtle argumentation from the old-covenant Scriptures might suggest that its audience consisted of Jews who were quite familiar with and would understand such detailed discussion of biblical figures such as Cain, Abel, Noah, Abraham and Moses, and others mentioned in Hebrews 11, or of priestly figures such as Melchizedek, Levi and Aaron in Hebrews 7. This would also make sense of a whole host of details about the work of Levitical priests in the old-covenant tabernacle throughout chapters 8–10. Who else, it might be argued, would both know and care about all of these details other than a Jewish audience? Similarly, the intricate arguments that Hebrews uses, which sometimes depend on the exact wording of the old-covenant Scriptures in Greek translation (e.g. in Heb. 2:7, 9), might also suggest that the letter is written to a (Hellenistic) Jewish audience very familiar with

[1] See e.g. Wuest 1962: 46; Marshall 1975: 137; Weeks 1976: 79–80; Hughes 1977: 11; Bruce 1990: 6; Lindars 1991: 4; Ellingworth 1993: 80, 530; Salevao 2002: 113; Witherington 2007: 26, 55; Thomas 2008: 105, 120; Stedman 2009: 13; D. E. Johnson 2018: 21–22; Peterson 2020: 19; Schreiner 2020: 7; Cara 2024: 16.

[2] Lindars 1991: 4.

Septuagintal translations. In addition, the author's extensive concern for ways in which the ministry of Christ and the new covenant are superior to the old covenant are often thought to be most pertinent to an audience that is tempted to turn back to some pre-Christian or non-Christian form of Jewish belief and practice.[3] Otherwise, why would all of this detailed comparison between old and new covenants be relevant?

Revisionist criticisms

Despite how common the above view has been regarding the temptation that Hebrews addresses, it has also been strongly questioned in recent times by a growing number of scholars who both critique the past consensus and offer alternative interpretations in its place.[4] While there is certainly some diversity of viewpoint among these revisionist scholars, they have together made various observations about both Hebrews itself and past scholarship on Hebrews that are challenging and worthy of close consideration.

Regarding Hebrews itself, these revisionist scholars have pointed out several features of what the letter does or does not say that they believe undermine the traditional consensus and its assumptions. For example, in a general way, they point out that detailed scriptural argumentation does not in itself necessitate the conclusion that a document was written to a Jewish audience. After all, Galatians too argues in detail about biblical figures, texts and categories, yet its audience is clearly Gentile.[5] To assume that detailed concern for Scripture or God's covenants with Israel requires a Jewish audience therefore does not hold. To similar effect, revisionist scholars also point out that, unlike in an epistle such as Galatians where the threat of Christians 'Judaizing' is clearly at issue, Hebrews itself

[3] Formulating the argument in a slightly broader way, D. A. Carson and Douglas J. Moo (2005: 610) suggest that Hebrews' extended argument for the obsolescence of the old covenant makes sense only if the audience is either still trying to live under the old covenant or seeking to revert to it.

[4] Those who believe that the audience is *not* tempted to return to Judaism include Lane 1991: cxxvii, cxxv; deSilva 2000: 6, 19; Koester 2001: 72, 77; Eisenbaum 2005b: 216; Mitchell 2007: 13; 2011: 254–255; Schenck 2007: 40–41; 2019: 14; Thompson 2008: 7–8, 20; Hooker 2009: 190–191, 197; Mason 2010: 20; Gray 2011: 14; Whitlark 2014: 12–16, 49–76; Grindheim 2023: 32; Easter 2024: 124; Martin and Whitlark 2024: 350.

[5] Schenck 2019: 33. Similar issues are acknowledged by Gordon (2008: 12) and Peterson (2020: 15).

never even uses the terms 'Jew' or 'Gentile',[6] and it reflects no concern for the heavily contested practice of circumcision either.[7] In addition, they suggest that Hebrews does not concern itself with any active controversy over common Jewish distinctives related to kosher dietary practice, observance of holy days, or ceremonial washings.[8] In other words, they believe that the telltale indicators of a controversy between Christianity and non-Christian Judaism are simply lacking. Instead, when practices related to washings or food *are* mentioned in Hebrews (e.g. 6:2; 13:9–10), some revisionist scholars contend that these references still do not reflect an active concern that the audience might adopt non-Christian Jewish practices. They can instead be seen as referring to a wide array of other ablutionary or dietary practices present in the Greco-Roman world more generally, not necessarily Jewish ones,[9] or can be understood as the author's use of mere 'boilerplate' material of a generic kind, largely unrelated to any live issue within his audience's own experience.[10] As a result, while Hebrews does of course make arguments contrasting the old and new covenants, these scholars assert that clear indicators of a conflict between Christianity and non-Christian Judaism are simply not present in the letter, thereby undermining the notion that a possible return to Judaism is what elicits these old–new contrasts.

In addition, several revisionist scholars have argued against the past 'return to Judaism' consensus by emphasizing the lack of any clear exhortation regarding that danger within Hebrews' own discourse. Making a distinction between sections of exposition (or instructional content) and exhortation in Hebrews, they argue that, though Hebrews makes detailed arguments about the relative superiority of the new covenant to the old in its expositional sections, its exhortation sections (where the implications of these arguments are shown) never state that a return to Judaism or the synagogue should be avoided. Apparently, then, that is not the underlying reason why the author expounds on the covenants as he does.

Along these lines, Kenneth Schenck reviews both the expositional and exhortational content of Hebrews in some detail and says that the

---

[6] Eisenbaum 2005a: 2–3; Hays 2009: 153; Schenck 2019: 41.

[7] Hays 2009: 154.

[8] Ibid.; Eisenbaum 2005b: 235; Mason 2010: 18–20.

[9] Eisenbaum 2005b: 235. More recently, see Martin and Whitlark 2023.

[10] Koester 2001: 72; Schenck 2007: 41; Thompson 2008: 7–8; Mason 2010: 18–19. Similarly, Grindheim 2023: 32, 678.

evidence falls short of showing that a possible return to Judaism is of any direct concern in the letter. In the process, Schenck also asserts that the letter's exhortations should be considered the more direct and determinative evidence for reconstructing the audience's situation, with the expositional content providing only more indirect and less important evidence by comparison. With a particular focus on the exhortations in Hebrews, then, Schenck finds clear evidence of the audience being urged to continue forward in a Christian profession, including exhortations to 'pay attention' (2:1), 'hold fast' (3:6, 14), 'hold to the confession' (4:14; 10:23), 'bring to completion' (6:1), 'approach God with boldness for help' (4:16; 10:22), and not shrink to destruction but instead persist in faith (10:39; ch. 11). By contrast, he finds no clear evidence of exhortations against going backward to any other specific past form of belief and practice, and no clear polemical concern about a possible reliance on or return to Judaism.[11]

In a similar way, James Thompson also surveys the expositional and exhortational content of Hebrews and argues for the greater importance of the latter. In summary, he notes exhortations to the audience about drifting away (2:1), falling away (3:12), falling short (4:11), falling (6:6), sinning deliberately (10:26) and throwing away their confidence (10:35), all of which focus on the problem of not continuing forward with a Christian profession. What he does not find, however, is evidence identifying a specific alternative threat to the audience's continuation in the Christian faith that the audience is then warned to avoid.[12]

Using arguments like these, revisionist scholars therefore tend to insist that the purpose of Hebrews should be understood and formulated *positively*, with regard to what it urges the audience to do in continuing forward, rather than *negatively*, with regard to some perceived threat to which the audience might fall prey. As Thompson says, the evidence in Hebrews shows that 'the author is more concerned with the community's abandonment of the faith than with any alternative they might take'.[13] In this way, scholars conclude that the presence of a specific temptation to return to Judaism is simply never made clear in Hebrews, especially since

[11] See Schenck 2007: 26–41. For a direct statement that Hebrews is offering 'a polemic against Judaism', see Thomas 2008, esp. p. 105.

[12] Thompson 2008: 10. See similarly Lane 1991: cxxvii, cxxv; Isaacs 1992: 27; deSilva 2000: 17; Gray 2011: 14.

[13] Thompson 2008: 10.

a direct exhortation against such a return is nowhere to be found in what is otherwise a lengthy and carefully worded letter that does include many other kinds of express warnings within it.[14]

Revisionist proposals

Given these conclusions about what is *not* clearly evidenced in Hebrews and what temptation Hebrews is not addressing, revisionist scholars have gone beyond critiquing the return-to-Judaism interpretation itself to critiquing past Hebrews scholarship as a whole, by identifying the assumptions or biases which they believe have helped to create and undergird the older, return-to-Judaism consensus. Especially prominent within such criticisms has been a notable concern with supersessionism, a topic around which many of the revisionist views have overtly been framed. This includes maintaining that past scholars have at least implicitly seen Israel, the texts of Israel's Scriptures, or God's historic relationship with Israel as something now rejected or annulled with the coming of Christ.[15] Some have also articulated a more specific concern regarding the presence of anti-Semitism or anti-Jewishness within past scholarship.[16] Moreover, concern has repeatedly been expressed about negative or disparaging characterizations of Judaism over against Christianity in past scholarship. Richard Hays, for example, begins an influential essay on the topic this way:

> Does the Letter to the Hebrews articulate a supersessionistic theology? For a long time, there has been a clear consensus among interpreters that it is so, that Hebrews emphatically represents Judaism as a religion now rejected and replaced by Christianity.[17]

Similarly, Alan Mitchell seeks to counteract a supersessionistic interpretation that 'promotes Christianity as a replacement for Judaism'.[18] Of special

---

[14] Mason 2010: 9.

[15] Eisenbaum 2005a: 1; Hays 2009: 151; Mitchell 2011: 251.

[16] Mitchell, for example (ibid.), says that supersessionism leads to anti-Semitism.

[17] Hays 2009: 151. In a refreshing instance of self-deprecation, which embodies the non-triumphalistic spirit that his essay also seeks to commend, Hays then disarmingly goes on to cite his own assessment of Hebrews at an earlier point in his career as an example of past scholarship that simply assumed Hebrews was supersessionistic in its theology.

[18] Mitchell 2011: 254.

concern in this regard is 'a triumphalist attitude about Christianity',[19] an interpretative stance by scholars that 'denigrates' or 'disparages' Judaism,[20] and a view of Christianity and Judaism in which the former 'stand[s] in a position of secure superiority' to the latter.[21] Along with this, revisionist scholars suggest that the perspective of past scholarship has been unduly influenced by the later experience of the church (long after the apostolic period) when 'Christianity' and 'Judaism' existed as two clearly defined and separate entities, a state of affairs which they believe simply did not pertain in any clear way in the first or second century when Judaism and Christianity had not yet decisively parted ways.[22]

With such concerns in mind, revisionist scholars have concluded that the return-to-Judaism consensus was actually the product of assumptions or biases embedded within past scholarship, because Hebrews itself provides no clear evidence to support it.[23] According to Pamela Eisenbaum, 'There is precious little within the body of Hebrews itself to indicate that the addressees are in danger of "back-sliding into Judaism."'[24] Similarly, Marie Isaacs states that Hebrews 'gives no indication as to what constituted a threat to [the audience's] faith' or 'what they might be reverting to'.[25] Going further, Eric Mason maintains that in Hebrews 6 'one finds no hint that going back to an earlier kind of faith [i.e. Judaism] is the problem' and that the warning passages of Hebrews never imply that 'regression to some sort of inferior religious commitment' is at issue.[26] Indeed, while past scholarship has sometimes simply assumed that returning to Judaism is the temptation the audience faced, Mason believes this assumption is belied by the fact that 'the author [of Hebrews] never *explicitly* says that this is his point'; it is hard to believe that this would be the case in such a long and carefully written letter if it were his actual concern.[27] Importantly, Mason even insists that 'the author of Hebrews never

[19] Ibid. 266.

[20] Ibid. 256; Mason 2010: 13, 16; cf. Schenck 2019: 197; Lane 1991: cxxv–cxxvi.

[21] Hays 2009: 172.

[22] Ibid. 153–155; Eisenbaum 2005b: 233; Schenck 2019: xii–23.

[23] Eisenbaum 2005a: 1; 2005b: 214, 216; Hays 2009: 151–154; Schenck 2019: vii.

[24] Eisenbaum 2005b: 216.

[25] Isaacs 1992: 27.

[26] Mason 2010: 9–10.

[27] Ibid. 9.

utilizes the theme of reversion to an earlier existence'.[28] Interestingly, some scholars who adopt the traditional consensus position agree that Hebrews never directly *says* that reversion to Judaism is the temptation the audience faces, yet they believe that the letter implies this is the case through its content and tone.[29] But, for revisionist scholars, the lack of overt statements about a return to Judaism amounts to a critical weakness, betraying the influence of unhelpful or even anti-Jewish assumptions that skew perception of the letter as a whole and also of its intended purpose.

So, then, given their criticisms of past scholarship and its assumptions, revisionist scholars have sought to offer better readings of the evidence in Hebrews, leading to various alternative proposals. In the process of their rereading, these scholars have offered a variety of fresh observations and interpretative suggestions about Hebrews that warrant careful attention.

One particularly important suggestion is that Hebrews is not actually designed to keep people from going *back* to a past form of religiosity (Judaism) at all, but just to help them move *forward*. Often this proposal is joined to the idea that Hebrews is a response to the existential crisis created by the destruction of the Jewish temple in Jerusalem in AD 70. If so, Hebrews should be understood not as an effort to dissuade people from going back to the old-covenant Levitical system, which was impossible to utilize anyway with the temple gone, but instead as an effort to persuade them how they can possibly continue forward in such new, otherwise devastating circumstances.[30] According to Eisenbaum, Hebrews represents an effort to preserve and continue a heritage that Christianity holds in common with Judaism in response to a commonly experienced problem. The issue, then, is not whether to go back, but how to survive.[31] Along with this, revisionist interpretations often emphasize the likelihood or necessity of Hebrews' being written at a later date (certainly after AD 70 but perhaps even sometime in the second century),[32] and some surmise

[28] Ibid.

[29] See e.g. Salevao (2002: 113), who bases his traditional conclusions on indirect evidence such as the 'general tenor' of the letter and the 'whole orientation' of its argument, which provide a 'strong inference'.

[30] Isaacs 1992: 67; Eisenbaum 2005a: 1–2; 2005b: 233; Mitchell 2011: 251, 254.

[31] Eisenbaum 2005b: 217. See also Schenck 2019: 14, 21.

[32] Mitchell (2011: 266) notes a later, post-70 AD date as one of two key characteristics of the revisionist reassessment of Hebrews. See also Eisenbaum 2005b: 225–226, 230; Schenck 2007: 197; 2019: 21; Mason 2010: 16.

that it is most likely written to a Gentile audience as well.[33] Within this context, drawing contrasts between the old and new covenants also does not imply disparagement of anything inherent to the old priestly system.[34] Instead, it is simply an argument for survival and continuation, for which both Christians and non-Christian Jews were seeking a rationale once the temple was gone.

Insights and problems in revisionist scholarship

On reflection, revisionist scholars have offered interpreters a lot to think about, including by making some careful observations about past Hebrews scholarship and about the text of Hebrews itself. Yet some problems appear in their alternative proposals too. It will therefore be useful to consider both strengths and weaknesses in their proposals – a process which will also help us to identify key factors that can sharpen our own reconsideration of the evidence in Hebrews in subsequent chapters.

Among the clearly helpful emphases and proposals put forward by revisionists, several components stand out. First, revisionist emphasis on the need to question interpretative assumptions in scholarship, and to seek to notice where interpreters fill gaps in their own views by importing foreign considerations from outside the text, is especially salutary. Indeed, revisionist scholarship helps to show in a striking fashion how one and the same set of data in a text can potentially be construed in several different ways, each of which can have a significant degree of plausibility depending on a person's other assumptions. In this way, revisionists helpfully highlight the need for interpreters to stick more closely to the text and to be sure they are grounding their key claims in the text itself, rather than making unwarranted leaps in argumentation. Why, for example, should it be assumed that Gentile readers would not be interested in the fate of the temple,[35] or in close analysis of old-covenant figures, institutions and the like? Or why do interpreters (on both sides) tend to assume

[33] Those proposing a Gentile audience include Schenck 2007: 193–194; 2019: viii, 38; Gray 2011: 14; Mitchell 2011: 254. However, Isaacs (1992: 67) and Hays (2009: 165) still believe the audience is more likely Jewish, and Eisenbaum (2005b: 232–233) and Mason (2010: 20) both believe the ethnicity of the audience is not essential to understanding the book.

[34] Mason 2010: 13, 15.

[35] Schenck 2019: 29.

that the Jewish or Gentile make-up of the audience is of great importance to the letter, when the text itself makes no overt use of those categories? Are interpreters importing their own concerns into the text without warrant? Given the clear possibility of our doing this, there is particular value in the emphasis that many revisionists put on reconstructing 'the text's own narrative world',[36] as evidenced within the pages of Hebrews itself. New Testament texts display a great deal of diversity among themselves, which is easy to overlook or underplay by unintentionally conflating them with one another. This conflation is unfortunate because, in actual fact, the worlds of thought evidenced in Hebrews and Galatians, to name just two examples, are in many ways quite different from each other. So it is crucial for us to ask what does and does not fit within the discrete symbolic thought-world of Hebrews itself as we read it.

Second, revisionist interpreters have pushed for a nuanced view of how to relate ancient Judaism and Christianity, especially in the first century. In part, this means appreciatively recognizing the inalienably Jewish roots of Christianity, which Hebrews strongly highlights in various ways, and therefore the complexity of questions related to when, where and how Christian belief and practice (including as represented in Hebrews) were built directly upon and remained largely continuous with the broad milieu of first-century Jewish thought. Especially important in this regard is the revisionist effort to avoid an unfairly polemical or even disparaging account of non-Christian Jewish thought and practice. Indeed, a concern to take a positive, constructive view of the old covenant's relation to the new is quite deeply woven into Hebrews itself. Certainly, Hebrews is not rejecting or negating Israel but is instead engaging with and carrying forward its heritage,[37] using categories that are thoroughly Jewish to see the audience as existing in some kind of continuity with Israel.[38] So, then, whatever contrasts the letter may make between the old and new covenants, these are still placed within a framework of appreciatively and constructively comparing what is good with what is better, not what is bad with what is good, as will be further reflected upon below.

However, alongside these and other useful aspects of revisionist

---

[36] Hays 2009: 153–154. See also Kenneth Schenck's earlier description of a method for unpacking 'The Story World of Hebrews' in Schenck 2003, esp. pp. 5–23.

[37] Hays 2009: 155.

[38] Gordon 2008: 27–29; Schenck 2019: 197. For an exposition of the Jewish roots of some key themes in Hebrews, see also Moffitt 2021; Martin and Whitlark 2024: 351–358.

interpretation, some problem areas must also be noted. The following stand out for particular mention here.

First, despite their helpful insistence on close readings of Hebrews and attention to its internal thought-world, revisionist proposals still often rely on extrinsic commitments of their own that stand in tension with Hebrews' language or thematic emphases. The most prominent example consists of their frequent heavy emphasis on the destruction of the temple as the crucial contextual factor for understanding the letter. Importantly, despite Hebrews' extensive interest in priests, priesthoods, tabernacles and sacrifices, it never mentions the temple itself (speaking only about the old-covenant tabernacle or tent throughout its pages) and certainly never mentions the temple's destruction, whether the earlier destruction by Babylon in 586 BC or the subsequent one perpetrated by Rome in AD 70. And to be clear, the point I am making here is not to engage in argumentation for or against a post-70 AD dating of the letter as a whole, which is really not germane at this juncture, but instead to point out that, whether the Roman destruction of the temple was already past or still in the future when Hebrews was written, that historical event (or the one like it in 586 BC) is never once mentioned or even clearly hinted at in the letter itself, whether prospectively or retrospectively. As a result, a significant irony emerges when revisionists argue against a return-to-Judaism interpretation of Hebrews on the grounds that such a return is never *overtly* mentioned in Hebrews (a claim that we will actually disagree with later below), but then argue in favour of the destruction of the temple as the decisive factor for interpretation when that topic is clearly not *overtly* mentioned in the letter either.[39] This methodological inconsistency is quite telling, particularly since some revisionists make such strong claims about traditional interpretative biases influencing interpretation.

A similar problem emerges when some revisionist authors note that Hebrews never uses terms for 'Jew' and 'Gentile' and claim this silence as part of the reason why a conflict between Christianity and Judaism is not a live issue for the audience, but then go on to insist that the audience of Hebrews must be ethnically Gentile. Evidence of silence used against one interpretation is thereby ignored for the sake of another.

[39] For example, Schenck (2019: 195) argues that Hebrews is not a polemic against the temple cult because that is never stated, but asserts that Hebrews is instead 'an admonition to move beyond distress over the loss of the temple' before then acknowledging that 'the Jerusalem temple [is] never explicitly mentioned' in it.

Again, a very similar problem emerges with revisionist interpretations that require a late dating of Hebrews. On the one hand, it is fair to point out that some evidence for an early date of Hebrews (such as the use of present-tense verbs to describe the operation of the Levitical cult in 8:4, 13; 9:8–10; 13:10) is potentially ambiguous and therefore not conclusive. But on the other hand, to then turn and insist on a late date for Hebrews as crucial for reconstructing the letter's central purpose and message claims a degree of certainty in the other direction that evidence in the text *also* does not afford.

By contrast, given the nature of the evidence that the letter itself offers, readings that do not rely heavily on one narrow reconstruction of date and audience but remain open to a broad range of possibilities would seem to be both wiser and more fair. Unfortunately, those contending that scholarly assumptions extrinsic to Hebrews undergird the return-to-Judaism paradigm have frequently ended up relying quite heavily on their own set of assumptions, which are arguably even less supported by the text.

Second, in addition to over-reliance on various interpretative assumptions that stand in tension with the text, revisionist interpretations sometimes require too narrow a set of evidence for saying that Hebrews seeks to distance its audience from other, non-Christian Jewish practices. In a survey of recent scholarship, Mitchell notes that a key part of the revisionist argument has been the observation that no specific, identifiable form of first-century Judaism is described or responded to in Hebrews. In his view, this helps to show that Judaism is not actually what the letter seeks to counter or replace.[40] Similarly, Eisenbaum states that Hebrews is more interested in 'a theological issue' than with 'problems of practice in a particular community'.[41] She therefore also notes that the letter's construction of its own context is '*suspiciously* lacking in information related to questions of who, what, where, when, etc.'[42] and that 'there is nothing in Hebrews that indicates the addressees practice some form of Judaism'.[43] The point, then, is essentially that, since Hebrews lacks enough detailed specificity to show that it is in debate with any particular, known form of

[40] Mitchell 2011: 266.

[41] Eisenbaum 2005b: 222.

[42] Ibid. 231; emphasis original.

[43] Ibid. 234.

first-century Judaism, it must not really be concerned to distance its audience from Judaism at all.

To be sure, it is important to read Hebrews on its own terms, to note how concern for topics such as circumcision and holy days (which are important for defining some early Christian controversies with Judaism) is not evident in this letter, and so to avoid conflating Hebrews with Galatians or other Pauline texts. At the same time, though, Mitchell and Eisenbaum make an assumption here that a high degree of *specificity* about a particular Jewish sect is needed for Hebrews to have any interest in distancing its audience from non-Christian Jewish beliefs or practices of some kind. This requirement of detailed specificity seems unnecessary and without specific evidentiary basis.

While it is true that Hebrews does not enter into an argument in enough specific detail to allow us to identify any particular *species* of contemporary Judaism as a threat to its audience, this does not negate the possibility of its making broader arguments against a return to pre-Christian Jewish belief or practice as a *genus*.[44] In this regard, when Eisenbaum states that Hebrews is not seeking to supersede Judaism but only the Levitical cult,[45] this potentially poses a false alternative. After all, an argument such as the one Hebrews makes – against the necessity or sufficiency of the Levitical cult and in favour of the better mediation provided by an altogether different priesthood (Melchizedekian) in a different location (heaven) with a different sacrifice (Christ's own) – surely mitigates against any form of non-Christian Jewish practice that either still relied on the temple cult as essential or was developed as an extension or application of Levitical ceremonial purity. In this way, even if Hebrews was not written to comment directly on any specific strand of Judaism,[46] this does not preclude it from making a broader and more all-encompassing argument against all forms of Jewish belief for which Christ was not seen as the sole ultimate fulfilment of God's past ways with Israel. On reflection, then, to insist that the author of Hebrews must argue against a specific sect of Judaism in order to argue against non-Christian Judaism at all places an

[44] Lane (1991: cxxxv) makes this distinction too, contending that, although early Christians saw themselves as part of (i.e. not separate from) Judaism, Hebrews nevertheless argues that the audience cannot turn the clock back to how things were before their Christian confession.

[45] Eisenbaum 2005a: 4–5.

[46] Ibid.

unwarranted restriction on how the author must go about making a case for a certain broad outcome if he wished to do so.

With this distinction in mind, it should be noted that the argument to be made below will focus particularly on the question of whether the audience of Hebrews is tempted to return to the *old covenant* rather than to 'Judaism' as such. This way of putting the question fits better with the covenantal categories that Hebrews itself uses, thereby respecting the terms within which the author casts his own argumentation.

Third and relatedly, revisionist interpretations sometimes discount the available evidence suggesting that the author is in fact seeking to distance his audience from some form of non-Christian Jewish practice. For example, Eisenbaum suggests when reading Hebrews 6:2 that washings or ablutions, mentioned in that verse, were common across many sectors of Greco-Roman society and were therefore not necessarily Jewish.[47]

However, this gives too little weight to the larger context in Hebrews, where the washings mentioned later are specifically from the old covenant, which the author says cannot perfect the conscience of the worshipper (9:9–10). Later in Hebrews, it is also the diverse ceremonies of the old covenant that are specifically contrasted with the washing provided in the new (10:22). In these ways, Hebrews is more concerned with ablutionary practices associated with the old covenant than Eisenbaum and others have allowed.

More importantly, while debates over the details of Jewish dietary provisions or kosher laws do not appear to be in dispute in Hebrews, nevertheless Hebrews 13:9–10 does reinforce a distinction between the food fellowship enjoyed by the audience itself and that which is associated with the old-covenant tabernacle – and it does so in a way that has clear contemporary relevance for the audience's own continued practice. In this regard, 13:9 warns the audience not to be led astray by strange teachings about foods, which do not benefit those devoted to them. Then verse 10 underscores how the members of the Hebrews's audience eat at an altar from which those serving the old-covenant tent have no right to eat. In this way, the author directly distinguishes Christian food fellowship from some other form of Jewish (particularly priestly) eating associated with service at the old-covenant tent. So, then, though these verses do not provide great detail, and though the threat of strange teaching and

[47] Eisenbaum 2005b: 235; cf. Hays 2009: 154.

food may be a distant rather than an immediate one for the audience,[48] these verses nevertheless seek to assure the audience about the value and sufficiency of their own communal food fellowship in contrast to an alternative one associated with the old covenant – one which others in their environment practised instead and by which the audience of Hebrews should not be misled. In this way, the admonitions in 13:9–10 also relate closely to some of the central themes found in the body of Hebrews, showing that the content of these verses should not just be marginalized in relation to the rest of the letter.[49]

Regarding both washings and foods, then, revisionist denials that Hebrews seeks to distance its audience from other contemporary Jewish practices seem overstated. Especially in Hebrews 13:9–10, a sociological distinction is reinforced between the audience of Hebrews, on the one hand, and some other contemporary Jewish eating practices associated with the old-covenant priesthood, on the other.

Fourth, revisionist arguments are sometimes based on overly simplistic assertions about how Christianity and various forms of Judaism may relate. For example, Mason argues concerning the food in Hebrews 13:9–10: 'Even if Jewish food laws are in view, one need not see this as proof that [the author's] major point is a rebuttal of Judaism. Rather, food is mentioned as deficient compared to grace'.[50] The logic of this statement relies, at least in a general way, on the view championed by E. P. Sanders that ancient Judaism is itself a religion of grace, just like Christianity. In the light of that, Mason is arguing that, since the foods in Hebrews 13:9 are contrasted with grace, they are not being contrasted with Judaism, which also believed in grace. As Schenck puts it when setting up his own global reassessment of Hebrews, Hebrews cannot be critiquing Judaism because 'Judaism affirmed the grace of God'.[51]

Yet, as important as it is to be fair and nuanced in one's descriptions of Judaism (especially given how Christian scholarship has a history of not doing this) and so to acknowledge the grace-filled nature of Second

---

[48] Contra Lindars (1991: 9–10), who takes the alternative altar fellowship mentioned in 13:9–10 to indicate the central and immediate threat to which Hebrews as a whole is addressed.

[49] Contra Mason 2010: 17–20. By comparison, Hays (2009: 154 n. 8) acknowledges that Heb. 13:9 may well be referring to a contemporary Jewish controversy over foods in the audience's own environment.

[50] Mason 2010: 18.

[51] Schenck 2019: vii.

Temple Jewish thought, scholarship since Sanders has also continued to emphasize the diversity of views present within Judaism, including on the topic of grace itself and of what precise role grace plays within the thought of different Jewish groups or authors.[52] Included within this diversity is the fact that, while both Judaism and Christianity constructed grace-based soteriologies, they did not do so in exactly the same ways. As a result, one person with a grace-based system of thought may still view another person's grace-based system of thought as having an *insufficient* construction of grace and therefore of being improperly or not *adequately* grace-based at all.

So, then, one cannot simply conclude that a contrast between grace and foods necessarily contains no contrast between Christian and non-Christian Jewish thought or practice, as Mason too quickly asserts. To the contrary, more distinctions are necessary in order to be fair to the diversity found in the first-century context.

To similar effect, Mason argues that Hebrews 13:10 is not polemicizing Judaism but is instead simply making an earth–heaven contrast. Here again, this analysis understates the situation as the author of Hebrews would see it. After all, saying that God's Messiah provides permanently effective priestly mediation in the archetypal tabernacle in heaven, rather than the one on earth, surely mitigates against the necessity of utilizing any separate, lesser form of Levitical mediation or outward purification associated with the earthly tent. It is far from clear, then, that the earth–heaven contrast employed by the author of Hebrews is not intended to help distance Hebrews' audience from contemporary non-Christian cultic or food practices. To the contrary, much about Hebrews' argumentation makes this a distinct possibility.

Fifth, revisionist arguments against seeing Judaism as a temptation in Hebrews also need to be clearer on the topic of supersessionism itself, particularly regarding how supersessionism itself is not *necessarily* anti-Jewish and how arguing against a return to Judaism does not *necessarily* entail a disparagement of non-Christian Jewish thought and practice as such. While concern to recognize and uproot anti-Semitic or anti-Jewish thought is very important and necessary,[53] not least given the history of modern New Testament interpretation's severe failings in this regard,

[52] Barclay 2015.

[53] Mitchell 2011: 251.

great care is still needed when analysing Hebrews' arguments lest we paint with too broad and undifferentiated a brush, eliding certain legitimate interpretative options in the process. For example, Mason argues as follows:

> Clearly the Christian author of Hebrews intends to present Jesus as superior to what came before him; this would hardly be a Christian text if Jesus were merely presented as *like* his predecessors. Must, however, the author of Hebrews also be understood as having the parallel goal of disparaging Judaism and thus discouraging his readers against either returning or clinging to that which Jesus has surpassed?[54]

While acknowledging that Hebrews does see Jesus as superior to the old-covenant cult, Mason nevertheless presents the interpretative options in a way that makes any argument for not returning to the old covenant entail *disparagement* of what came before. Yet such an entailment is by no means necessary, as other revisionist authors recognize more clearly. For example, Richard Hays observes that supersessionism itself is not inherently anti-Jewish, since much early Jewish literature is supersessionistic regarding the Old Testament or Levitical cult.[55] Similarly, Eisenbaum notes: 'from our modern perspectives, two religious systems successfully "superseded" the religion of ancient Israel: Rabbinic Judaism and Christianity.'[56] It is important to recognize, then, that supersession actually can be and often is a very Jewish motif, not something inherently anti-Jewish.

A related problem appears when Mason interweaves statements that Hebrews is not arguing against 'going back to an *earlier* kind of faith'[57] with statements that it is not arguing against 'regression to some sort of *inferior* religious commitment'.[58] Yet the terms 'earlier' and 'inferior' need to be unpacked carefully here. While 'inferior' could be freighted with critically condescending or dismissive overtones, this too need not be so. Something inherently bad is of course inferior to something good.

[54] Mason 2010: 13.

[55] Hays 2009: 154 n. 10.

[56] Eisenbaum 2005a: 4–5.

[57] Mason 2010: 10; emphasis added.

[58] Ibid. 9; emphasis added.

But something good is also inferior to (i.e. lesser than) something better, and it is especially this latter kind of 'inferiority' that Hebrews often seeks to prove regarding the relation of the old covenant to the new, as Mason himself also notes.[59]

In fact, it is quite possible for Hebrews to be very appreciative of the old covenant as a good, gracious provision of God given to bless his people for a time, and yet also to see it as now surpassed by something greater and therefore *not* something to which a Christian should return. Readers of Hebrews can and should affirm several things at once. On the one hand, it is of utmost importance that Christians not be complacent and self-satisfied[60] or view *themselves* as superior to non-Christian Jews. It is also vital for Christians to see their religious lives as threatened by sin – indeed, to see their own present situation on analogy to the situation of the old-covenant wilderness generation and so to see the instruction in Hebrews as something that engages with and carries forward a specifically Jewish heritage.[61] On the other hand, arguments for the superiority of the new covenant to the old or against going back to pre-Christian (or non-Christian) forms of Jewish belief and practice do not necessarily involve arrogance or anti-Jewishness. Instead, more options need to be considered when addressing the complexity of Hebrews' argument about the old covenant being fulfilled in the new, and this is especially true when seeking to define the precise nature of the temptation faced by Hebrews' original audience.

Further reflection and remaining questions

On reflection, the arguments that recent revisionist scholars have made against saying that the audience of Hebrews was tempted by Judaism do provide probing and helpful criticisms of past scholarship and its assumptions in various ways. Of particular value is their emphasis on listening carefully to Hebrews and allowing its internal thought-world to come to life on its own terms, rather than controlling it through our own, extrinsic assumptions. In this regard, revisionist critiques of past scholarship can

[59] Ibid. 15.

[60] Hays 2009: 172.

[61] Ibid. 166.

no doubt help to clear the interpretative air of some exegetical preconceptions that have tended to cloud past discussions and so create a context for fresh observation in their place.

Yet at the same time, revisionist criticisms and counterproposals often seem to go too far in various respects, offering alternative constructions of Hebrews' context and message that also sit in tension with important aspects of the letter's own content. As a result, the greatest value of their work especially seems to consist in offering a robust call for careful textual reconsideration, including on the crucial topic of what exactly Hebrews does or does not indicate about the nature of the temptation that its audience faces.

Several crucial questions therefore come to the surface for further examination as we continue our probing of the letter. Does Hebrews only argue in favour of moving forward? Or does it also argue against going back to elements of pre-Christian belief and practice associated particularly with the old covenant? In addition, is an answer to these questions available only from indirect inference from Hebrews' teaching sections, or does the skilled author of such a long sermon ever overtly warn the audience against the danger of going back to the old covenant in terms that they should have understood? Subsequent chapters will provide fresh answers to these questions.

Before turning directly to those topics, though, another controversy in past scholarship must be surveyed first, not about the nature of the temptation that the audience faces but about the nature of the central warning that the author issues in response to it. While the subject of this second controversy is logically connected to the first, scholarship about it has actually grown up separately and warrants its own analysis, which we turn to now.

3

Old questions about the warning: is return to repentance impossible?

If the question of what problem or temptation Hebrews addresses has been a matter of debate in recent scholarship, the additional question of what Hebrews says in response to that temptation has been even more heavily debated and for a much longer period of time. While many passages are relevant to addressing this second question, none has been more central to discussions than Hebrews 6:4–6, which Dennis Johnson calls 'the most troubling passage' in all of Hebrews.[1] There Hebrews says:

> For it is impossible to restore to repentance those having once been enlightened and having tasted the heavenly gift and having become partakers of the Holy Spirit and having tasted the good word of God and the powers of the coming age and having fallen away, since they are (re)crucifying to themselves the Son of God and exposing him to shame.

Over time, these words have proven to be a source of difficulty,[2] puzzlement[3] and numerous competing interpretations, even to the point of being considered 'infamous',[4] particularly for how they speak not just about the possibility of falling away itself but about the impossibility in

[1] D. E. Johnson 2018: 84.

[2] E.g. 'Most would agree that the meaning and application of the Hebrews warning passages is a difficult challenge for even the finest biblical scholars' (Gleason 2007: 377).

[3] E.g. 'It is no secret that Hebrews 6:4–6 has puzzled exegetes for centuries' (Verbrugge 1980: 61). 'For centuries Christians have been puzzled by Hebrews 6:4–6' (Grudem 2000: 133).

[4] Oberholtzer 1988: 319.

at least some circumstances of a person's then being restored again to repentance. As Roger Nicole puts it:

> Intimately tied to interpretation [of Hebrews] are difficult questions to which perhaps no definitive answer may be forthcoming here on earth: Who are the people to whom the author refers? What is the sin that they have committed and which places them beyond recovery? How can such a situation be diagnosed with certainty in this world . . .?[5]

Of particular concern for the purposes of the present study, do Hebrews 6:4–6 teach a kind of 'one and done' view of apostasy, wherein at least some people who fall away from their Christian profession of faith can never return to it again and be saved? And if they do not teach this, then what can the author's strong language be properly and fairly understood to mean instead?

To be sure, the attention these verses have received is a subset of the attention that has been given to other things, including the so-called 'warning passages' in Hebrews in general (most notably 2:1–4; 3:12–14; 4:1, 11–13; 6:1–8; 10:26–31; 12:15–17, 25),[6] as well as broader theological topics such as historical debates between Calvinism and Arminianism,[7] and related issues such as election by God, the perseverance of true Christians, and assurance of salvation.[8] Yet, even within the complexity of those broader discussions, Hebrews 6:4–6 stand out as an especially challenging set of verses due in particular to the note of finality that they seem to sound, namely that in certain situations or for certain people (however those should be defined) being restored to repentance after falling away

[5] Nicole 1975: 355; cf. 361.

[6] For example, Oberholtzer's own essay (1988), just cited, is part of a series of five articles in *Bibliotheca Sacra* on the warning passages. See also the synthetic concern for all the warning passages in McKnight 1992: 21–59; Grudem 2000; Bateman 2007; Thomas 2008; Oropeza 2011.

[7] For an overview and critique of some interpretation focusing on this debate, see Oropeza 2011: 82–83. For a more extensive survey of the history of interpretation of the warning passages culminating in debates between Calvinism and Arminianism, which debates and the alternatives posed in them are then taken as interpretatively central for exegetical reconsideration, see Thomas 2008: 25–96.

[8] See, for example, how interest in the passage is framed by Marshall 1975: 137–157; Nicole 1975; McKnight 1992; Grudem 2000: 133–134; Emmrich 2003: 88. Persistent interest in whether the experiences listed in 6:4–5 must necessarily describe true Christians or not also shows how much interpretation of the passage is framed by these same concerns, e.g. Nicole 1975: 360–362; McKnight 1992: 43–55; Grudem 2000: 168; Osborne 2007: 128; Schreiner 2015: 182–183.

is overtly said to be 'impossible'. Accordingly, the problem that Gareth Cockerill sees in the warning passages of Hebrews as a whole no doubt arises most acutely from what Hebrews 6:4–6 particularly seem to say: '[these verses] are difficult, not just because they teach that it is possible to fall away from Christ, but also because they teach a falling from which there is *no return*.'[9]

However, despite the large volume of attention that these verses have received in the past, a close look at past interpretations shows significant weaknesses in their explanations, leaving the impression that perhaps the author's point in these verses has not yet been adequately identified and explained. Of particular importance is the inability of interpreters to account clearly and persuasively for the details of the author's own word-choice in these verses. A closer look at past explanations of the passage will help to detail where the problems lie, and it will also help to establish some useful parameters for developing a more persuasive, alternative interpretation thereafter.

Past interpretations and their weaknesses

When surveying past scholarship, eight distinct views of the warning in Hebrews 6:4–6 can be identified. While they each have strengths, they also betray key weaknesses that make them unpersuasive.

1 Christ alone

Perhaps the most common interpretation of Hebrews 6:4–6 and the impossibility of repentance is to view these verses as saying that, for the author of Hebrews, there is no salvation apart from Christ and therefore those rejecting him are destined for judgment. Since the apostates in the passage are rejecting Christ, whose atoning work is the only grounds for salvation in Hebrews, there is therefore no hope for them. Paul Ellingworth, for example, summarizes the reason for the impossibility

[9] Cockerill 2007: 257; emphasis added. In fact, while some would maintain that Heb. 10:19–39 generates the greater theological challenge (McKnight 1992: 23 n. 4), most interpreters have found the comparable statement about apostasy in 10.26 (that there no longer remains a sacrifice for sins for some people) to be conceptually much simpler to explain. E.g. Solari 1970: 155; Marshall 1975: 149; Hughes 1977: 419; Attridge 1989: 293; Bruce 1990: 261; Ellingworth 1993: 531, 533; L. T. Johnson 2006: 261; Witherington 2007: 288; Schreiner 2020: 324.

of repentance this way: 'once Christ and his sacrifice have been rejected, there is nowhere else to turn.'[10] Similarly, Buist Fanning explains the impossibility of repentance on the basis of the finality of Christ's own sacrifice, which logically entails 'the consequent hopelessness of one who knowingly rejects' that final sacrifice. No provision for sin is available to a person other than Christ.[11] Again, Harold Attridge says that Christ's sacrificial death is 'the bedrock on which the "foundation" (6:1) of repentance is built. Those who reject this necessary presupposition of repentance simply, and virtually by definition, cannot repent.'[12]

However, while this 'salvation-in-Christ-alone interpretation', as it might be called, states something true as far as it goes regarding salvation, its explanation of Hebrews' warning passages and especially of Hebrews 6:4–6 is not fully satisfying. Certainly, in Hebrews a person who rejects Christ cannot be saved. But this assertion itself does not answer the key question regarding this passage: whether it is also impossible for that same person to stop rejecting Christ later, turn back to him again, be accepted and so still be saved. The real interpretative difficulty in Hebrews 6:4–6, then, is not whether Christ is necessary for salvation, which is quite commonly asserted throughout the New Testament, but whether under certain circumstances a person is no longer able (or allowed?) to turn back to him again and be restored to a right (saving) relationship with God. This more specific matter is something that the Christ-alone interpretation really does not address in any clear way.

In fact, Attridge's statement above indirectly points out how this interpretation really amounts to something of a truism: within the thought-world of Hebrews, it is indeed true 'virtually by definition', as Attridge says, that a person who is rejecting Christ's sacrificial death, which is the only means for forgiveness, cannot simultaneously be repentant and therefore saved.

But saying this much really just pushes the question back one step further, from whether one can repent and be saved without Christ, to whether a person who has once rejected Christ can ever return to him again. Is the latter also a part of what Hebrews 6:4–6 says is 'impossible', or not?

---

[10] Ellingworth 1993: 323.

[11] Fanning 2007: 184–185.

[12] Attridge 1989: 169. Others taking a similar view include Lane 1991: 142; Emmrich 2003: 90, 95; L. T. Johnson 2006: 128; Cockerill 2007: 289; Fanning 2007: 184–185; Thompson 2008: 163.

In addition, the inadequacy of the Christ-alone reading becomes even more evident when some scholars emphasize the notion of a temporal condition being present in Hebrews 6:6. This often involves taking the participial phrases in verse 6 temporally, so that repentance is said to be impossible 'while' or 'as long as' someone is crucifying the Son of God and upholding him to open shame.[13] But as Roger Nicole says in response to this view:

> Nobody can repent at all, let alone be renewed to repentance, while he persists 'in crucifying to himself the Son of God.' This is a truism too obvious to warrant statement, not to speak of the awesome solemnity of Heb 6.[14]

Surely the wording of Hebrews 6:4–6 is saying something more than that.

Some also try to support a Christ-alone interpretation by saying that conversion or repentance can only take place once for any person, since Christ's sacrifice itself was a 'once for all' event, as Hebrews clearly emphasizes. For example, Cockerill states: 'As [Christ] accomplished his work "once for all" (9:12, 26; 10:10), the person who has "once" (6:4) received the benefit of his work and then apostatizes in the manner described by Hebrews cannot be renewed.'[15] However, Craig Koester correctly points out the problem with this analysis:

> Logically, it is difficult to see why a singular act of atonement would mean that repentance must also be a singular act . . . To be sure, those who repudiate Christ's sacrifice have no other basis for repentance, but why cannot a person be restored by being brought to a renewed appreciation of Christ's sacrifice?[16]

Importantly, in this response Koester poses one of the most crucial questions at the heart of the interpretative challenge found in Hebrews 6:4–6 and in all of Hebrews' warning passages. The key issue presented by the epistle's strong wording is not why it is impossible to be saved when

[13] See e.g. Healy 2016: 120.

[14] Nicole 1975: 357 n. 2.

[15] Cockerill 2007: 290–291. Similarly, Weiss 1991: 345, 347, 537; Thompson 2008: 134.

[16] Koester 2001: 320. Koester's reasoning directly undermines the arguments found in Löhr 1994: 247–248; Salevao 2002: 259–260, 272–275, 288–289.

rejecting Christ, but whether it is impossible to return to Christ again after having rejected him and still be saved. Analysis of Hebrews must therefore go deeper than the Christ-alone interpretation itself does.

2 False convert

Other interpreters have sought to address the impossibility of repentance in Hebrews 6 by stating that those who fall away were not true Christians to begin with and so cannot return to repentance. Philip Hughes, for example, says: 'the whole issue of this passage may be said to revolve around the question whether the internal reality, to which the external rite [of baptism] is designed to testify, is truly present or not.'[17] Accordingly, if a person truly apostatizes, then they must not have been truly regenerate to begin with and so cannot repent.[18]

However, this 'false convert' interpretation, as it might be called, also has several problems. For one thing, it is not clear why, if an unregenerate person repented falsely before, it becomes impossible for him or her to turn to Christ and repent truly afterwards. In this regard, a false-convert interpretation really provides no better answer than the previous interpretation.

In addition, it is important to note how the language of the passage focuses on the impossibility of a person being restored 'again' to repentance (6:6). In itself, this word 'again' implies that the second repentance under consideration in these verses (which the passage says is impossible) is actually of the same essential nature as the first repentance that the people in the passage had already experienced before. As Nicole puts it, the people being discussed in these verses had a first experience of repentance 'which it would be essential to renew' if they were to be saved.[19] After all, 'if the repentance that these apostates had experienced were not truly godly sorrow . . . it is hard to see why it would be desirable to renew it' anyway.[20] In principle, then, the issue at hand in the passage does not seem to lie in the deficiency of the first repentance as such (otherwise, why try to be renewed to it anyway?), but in the fact that, though the first repentance had great value and would in theory be desirable to repeat, it

[17] Hughes 1977: 221.

[18] See also Mathewson 1999: 222–225; Fanning 2007: 218–219.

[19] Nicole 1975: 356.

[20] Ibid. 361.

is nevertheless impossible under the circumstances described for that to happen. In other words, the key issue in these verses is not why repeating the same repentance as before is not even worthwhile since it was a false repentance anyway, but why repeating the same repentance as before, though desirable in theory, is still said to be impossible to do.

In addition, this critical weakness in the false-convert interpretation suggests that the problematics of Hebrews 6:4–6 are not adequately articulated through a controlling interpretative interest in theological topics such as divine election, inward regeneration, and true or false conversion, with which many scholars have been preoccupied. As important as those topics are in some biblical texts, it seems apparent that other interpretative categories need to be primary when reading *this* passage, given the details of its wording. *More specifically, it is crucial for any interpretation of this passage to explain how a change in situation could come about for some people, from an original situation in which a repentance was experienced that was good and desirable in itself, to a new situation in which repentance of the same basic kind, while in theory still desirable, is also no longer possible or savingly efficacious.* Later in this study, I will suggest that Hebrews itself provides just the sort of conceptual apparatus needed to explain how such a situational change can in fact come about for some people.

3 Special kind of apostasy

Some have sought to deal with the challenges of Hebrews 6:4–6 by saying that the impossibility of repentance only pertains to people committing a specific kind of apostasy, not just apostasy in general.[21] A 'special apostasy' interpretation like this then allows interpreters to account for cases, both in Scripture and in the subsequent experience of the church, in which some apostates have apparently made a genuine return to the faith. Such restored apostates simply show, by their return, that they had not committed this particular, special kind of apostasy described in Hebrews 6.[22] By contrast, Hebrews 6 must be describing apostasy of some particularly heinous or problematic kind. On reflection, though, at least two problems emerge with this view.

[21] For views that emphasize the kind of apostasy involved in bringing about the impossibility of return, see Osborne 2007; Gordon 2008: 92–93.

[22] Osborne 2007: 115.

On the one hand, despite saying that only certain kinds of apostasy are permanent and cannot be recovered from, scholars have not been able to specify what particular kinds of apostasy those are.[23] The only clear thing seems to be that any apostates who do repent and return to Christ did not commit that kind of apostasy.[24] Yet this effectively amounts to saying that it is impossible for a person to repent of apostasy unless he or she does, a statement that hardly seems to bear the hortatory weight of the categorical statement of impossibility and the strong tone of warning found in Hebrews. Indeed, for the audience of Hebrews to take this warning with full seriousness, yet also to avoid just falling into despair about the possibility of committing some kind of worse sin, it seems as though the specific nature of the worse sin would have to be made clear in the context. Yet as scholarship repeatedly shows, that kind of clarity just does not seem to be available in the passage itself.

On the other hand, one of the main reasons that scholars have not been able to identify what special kind of apostasy Hebrews 6:4–6 supposedly mentions is the fact that the verses themselves describe the act of apostasy itself quite plainly, as involving someone who has experienced certain blessings in their life (listed in 6:4–5) and has then 'fallen aside' (παραπεσόντας / *parapesontas*). Naturally, such a simple description of the act of apostasy does not go far towards delineating one narrow kind of apostatizing over against others. Of course, the passage does also go on to emphasize some further reasons why the apostate cannot be restored, because this amounts to (re)crucifying Christ and publicly shaming him (6:6). Later in this study, it will be shown how the grammar of verse 6 suggests that it is not actually the apostasy itself that brings about these additional results. In the meantime, though, we need to appreciate how this description of further consequences does not actually narrow down the kind of apostasy in view very much. After all, any repudiation of a previous public profession of faith in Christ (which is the kind of profession that Hebrews clearly describes in 3:1; 4:14; 10:23) would inevitably hold Christ up to public shame. In itself, then, the further descriptions in 6:6 do not provide much specificity regarding one particular kind of apostasy.

In addition, evidence elsewhere in the New Testament goes against saying that, when someone rejected Christ in a public way, this in

[23] Marshall 1975: 151.

[24] Osborne 2007: 115. Cf. Cockerill 2007: 291.

itself made their restoration to Christ impossible later. To the contrary, Oropeza points to Romans 11:25–32, Galatians 6:1, James 5:19–20 and Jude 22–23 as teaching the opposite,[25] to which other passages could also be added (e.g. Luke 15). Indeed, at least one very prominent figure in the apostolic church, who agreed publicly and repeatedly with those who rejected Christ at his crucifixion, was also restored to Christ publicly later (John 21:15–19). And within the Pauline circle itself (to which the author of Hebrews likely has some connection [Heb. 13:23]), expelling a person from the Christian assembly due to flagrant immorality was in fact done for the ultimate purpose of saving that person (1 Cor. 5:4–5), and it was understood that failing to restore a person who was remorseful over their sin would inadvertently play into the schemes of the devil (2 Cor. 2:5–11). It also appears likely that even public figures who had made a shipwreck of their own faith (1 Tim. 1:19–20) and so had led others to reject the truth too (2 Tim. 2:17–18) were still among those who should be treated with gentleness in hopes that they might yet *repent*, escape the devil's snare and embrace the truth again (2:25–26).[26]

So, then, the generic nature of the language about falling away in Hebrews 6:6 and the evidence about restoration from sin elsewhere in the New Testament both go against saying that Hebrews 6:6 identifies a particular, unique sort of apostasy from which one cannot repent and be restored. The impossibility of repentance must therefore be explained in some other way.

4 Human impossibility

Some have sought to tone down the matter of the impossibility of repentance by interpreting the passage in relation to something that is impossible for *people* to bring about but not for *God*. Some apostates, it might be said, get to a point where they are beyond the reach of other people's efforts to restore them, even though God himself might still do so. J. Behm, for example, says that 'no human possibility exists of bringing [the apostate]

[25] Oropeza 2011: 96.

[26] Note, for example, the common threads regarding being captive to Satan and the corresponding need for instruction/correction (*paideuō* [1 Tim. 1:19; 2 Tim. 2:25; cf. 2 Tim. 2:23]) in each context. For further discussion on the connections between these passages, see Towner 2006: 547, 551, as well as similar emphases in Knight 1992: 424–425; Bassler 1996: 156–157; Witherington 2006: 340; Montague 2008: 174.

afresh to conversion'.[27] Similarly, Rudolf Schnackenburg surmises that, given the terrible nature of someone's falling away from God's grace into the dark abyss of unbelief ('in den finsteren Abgrund des Unglaubens'), no preacher or teacher of the faith would be able to call that person back to repentance and that, in fact, Hebrews does not seem to have much hope for an extraordinary intervention by God in that person's life either.[28]

Yet such an anthropological interpretation also creates some exegetical difficulties. For one thing, Behm acknowledges that repentance is always a gift from God, which means that it is *always* impossible to repent, humanly speaking. It is unclear, then, how the situation of the apostate in Hebrews 6 is any different from that of any other unbeliever in this respect. For another thing, the wording in Hebrews 6 itself does not qualify the impossibility anthropologically but is quite plain and categorical in its wording.[29] By comparison, other statements in Hebrews about something being 'impossible' certainly appear to be categorical in their nature and do not apply only to human impossibility (e.g. 6:18; 10:4; 11:6). It is not clear, then, why the statement in 6:6 should be taken to be any different from that.[30] As I. Howard Marshall observes, the context in Hebrews 6 'gives us no right to assert that there may be a special intervention of God to restore those whom men cannot restore'[31] and so limit what the passage seems to assert. To the contrary, both the wording and the larger context suggest that, in the instances being discussed, the kind of repentance in view here is truly and categorically – not just humanly – impossible, even though it had not been impossible before when they experienced it the first time.

5 Particular hardness

Others explain the matter of impossibility subjectively, saying that the aggravated internal condition of some apostates makes repentance impossible. F. F. Bruce, for example, says that the author of Hebrews here states 'a practical truth', namely that those 'who have shared the covenant privileges of the people of God, and then deliberately renounce

---

[27] Behm and Würthwein 1964–76: 4: 1006.

[28] Schnackenburg 1950: 10–11. See also Spicq 1952: 1: 175; Solari 1970: 153; Michel 1975: 246; Oberholtzer 1988: 323.

[29] Löhr (1994: 154–155, 287) rightly notes that Hebrews' statement of impossibility is not based on something subjective or psychological but on the very nature of things as God has established it.

[30] See discussion in Attridge 1989: 167, esp. n. 14. See also Salevao 2002: 270.

[31] Marshall 1975: 142.

them, are the *most difficult* persons of all to reclaim for the faith'. These people, he says, have effectively been immunized against Christianity by having experienced a weakened form of it. Accordingly, 'as a matter of human experience the reclamation of such people is, *practically speaking*, impossible'.[32] Similarly, Mitchell states: 'Anyone who has gone so far as to apostatize after having been previously enlightened has made it *virtually* impossible to repent again.'[33] Interestingly, Thomas Schreiner takes a similar position but bases it in a kind of foreknowledge on the author's part about the internal state that would result in some apostates:

> [The author] perceives that if [the readers] turn away from Christ, there will be no future repentance for them. It isn't the case that God would not and could not forgive them. Rather, the readers, if they repudiate Christ, will have no desire to return to him.[34]

However, any interpretation that focuses on the special hardness of the people described in Hebrews 6 also suffers from significant problems. For one thing, these interpretations once again depend heavily on assertions not found in the passage, which itself says nothing of the apostate's internal state in a way that shows it to be categorically worse than that of any other unbeliever. For another thing, as each of the above quotes shows, this view tends to hedge on the matter of impossibility itself, not so much saying that repentance is impossible but only that it is unlikely or particularly difficult. Yet this not only waters down the author's actual language about impossibility;[35] it also seems doubtful that the impossibility at issue here lies merely in the apostate's not desiring it, since the author later, in a somewhat different context, describes Esau greatly desiring an opportunity for repentance and even seeking that with tears but still not finding it (12:17).

6 Corporate rejection

Some have dealt with the matter of impossibility by suggesting that Hebrews 6 is not about individuals but rather groups. Such a corporate

[32] Bruce 1990: 144; emphasis added in each quotation.

[33] Mitchell 2007: 128. See also Wuest 1962: 52; Grudem 2000: 150; Stedman 2009: 75; D. E. Johnson 2018: 87; Peterson 2020: 155; Grindheim 2023: 315, 639; Cara 2024: 197, 384.

[34] Schreiner 2020: 180.

[35] Solari 1970: 75; Verbrugge 1980: 69; Attridge 1989: 167.

interpretation was especially advanced by Verlyn Verbrugge, who argued that the language regarding thorn-infested ground in Hebrews 6:7–8 evokes Old Testament imagery which shows that it is only the permanent rejection of the faith by various Christian *communities* (rather than individuals) that is being described in verses 4–6, and that the warning therefore involves divine rejection of certain communities, rather than individual Christians losing salvation.[36] Yet Verbrugge himself acknowledges that the parallel warning found in Hebrews 10:26 applies to individuals. Moreover, Scot McKnight points out clear language in 3:12–13; 4:1, 10–11; and 10:28–29 that helps to demonstrate the author's concern for the unbelief, apostasy and judgment of *individuals*, even in the immediate context leading up to Hebrews 6:4–6.[37]

7 Loss of rewards

A few have suggested that Hebrews 6 is not about loss of salvation but only loss of certain rewards for those who are still saved. For example, according to Thomas Oberholtzer, the passage describes Christians whose sin may result in 'divine discipline in this life and in loss of future rewards in the millennium'.[38] In a somewhat different direction, Randall Gleason believes that the warning concerns avoiding the judgment that is going to fall on the Jewish nation in the destruction of the temple in AD 70.[39] But Wayne Grudem critiques Oberholtzer's exegesis, showing that the ground itself (not just the thorns it produces) is to be burned in Hebrews 6:7–8,[40] and McKnight walks carefully through all the warning passages in Hebrews, showing that the consequence at issue in them is in fact eternal punishment.[41] The key distinction made in a 'loss of rewards' interpretation, between salvation itself and other lesser rewards, therefore seems to be unfounded, thereby constituting one more example of scholars relying on a category distinction that is extrinsic to Hebrews 6 and its context in an unsuccessful attempt to deal with the passage's difficult language about impossibility.

[36] Verbrugge 1980: 62. See also Weeks 1976: 79.

[37] McKnight 1992: 54. See also Grudem 2000: 150; Salevao 2002: 284; Osborne 2007: 127.

[38] Oberholtzer 1988: 319.

[39] Gleason 2007: 337.

[40] Grudem 2000: 151.

[41] McKnight 1992: 33–36. For further interaction and critique see Thomas 2008: 170–178.

8 Rhetorical overstatement

While the preceding views already help to indicate how difficult scholars have found the notion of impossibility in Hebrews 6, a further indication may be found in a recent increase in interpreters who believe that Hebrews 6:4–6 is simply a rhetorical overstatement that is meant to shock its readers but does not actually mean what it says. Several decades ago, James Solari concluded that the author's concern in the letter 'is not speculative but very practical. In this epistle, therefore, he does not teach the impossibility of repentance for apostates, but rather attempts to warn the readers against turning away from the Faith.'[42] More recently, Ben Witherington has said that the words in Hebrews 6:4–6 'were intended to have a specific emotional effect, not comment in the abstract about what is impossible'.[43] Similarly, Thompson says that the author is not concerned with church discipline or theoretical discussion of the fate of apostates; his rhetorical goal is simply to shock his readers.[44] Yet such hyperbolic interpretations also have critical weaknesses.

First, thinking just from a pastoral angle, the approach to soul-care being ascribed to Hebrews on such views is both problematic and troubling. How short-sighted would it be to record publicly and in writing the emphatically worded statement that repentance after apostasy is impossible, if that is not what the author really meant but was only a scare tactic? What should be said later to any who do in fact apostatize? 'Oh, well, I didn't really *mean* that; you can still come back'? And what would need to be said to those who remained faithful in the Christian assembly (perhaps in part due to fear about the warning in Heb. 6) after someone else has apostatized and then attempts to return? 'I was just exaggerating – we really should forgive and accept this person'? The pastoral approach imagined by the hyperbolic interpretation is either profoundly short-sighted, if the author had not thought through such basic contingencies, or bordering on manipulation and deception, if he had.

---

[42] Solari 1970: 124.

[43] Witherington 2007: 214.

[44] Thompson 2008: 124. See also deSilva: 2000: 240–244; Koester 2001: 320. For his part, deSilva (2000: 240–244) says that Heb. 6:4–6 simply states what people as clients should be told about apostasy being irrevocable, so they will be warned against it, while not binding God as patron if he wishes to show mercy anyway. This hybrid position suffers from the shortcomings of both the anthropological view and the rhetorical overstatement view.

Second, Koester supports a hyperbolic reading by saying that 'speakers in antiquity understood the *effect* of their words to be as important as their meaning', but in this particular case it is difficult to see how the 'effect' of the author's words would be anything other than the exact *opposite* of their apparent meaning. After all, though the author's purpose is no doubt practical and not merely 'speculative' or 'abstract', as some point out, still a prima facie reading of his words does seem to show him plainly asserting 'the impossibility of repentance for apostates' at least in some sense or for some situations. As a result, simply stating that the author does not really assert this seems more like a tacit admission that these verses remain difficult to understand than like a lucid explanation of what they actually do say and why they say it.

Further reflection and remaining questions

On reflection, a survey of past views regarding the impossibility of repentance especially highlights several things. First, it helps to illustrate just how much the notion of the impossibility of repentance remains a problem for scholarship to explain, which therefore makes a more satisfying interpretation highly desirable. In fact, given the extent of the disagreement among scholars and the apparent discomfort often expressed with the text's own wording, a substantially new effort to address the whole topic seems recommendable. Second, the survey also suggests that a more satisfying interpretation needs to deal straightforwardly not just with whether it is impossible for an apostate to have any hope for salvation while rejecting Christ (a question which does not probe deeply enough) but with whether or not it is impossible for an apostate, having once rejected Christ, to return repentantly to him again and be saved. Third, the survey also suggests that a particular focus for future work should be on the matter of *situational change*, that is, why the repentance that a person experienced before, which in theory would be desirable to repeat, is said to be impossible now. What specifically is the nature of the repentance mentioned here, and what specifically has changed that makes that repentance impossible to be restored again? Finally, the survey also emphasizes the need to focus more closely on Hebrews itself and to seek to derive interpretative distinctions and categories from within its own world of thought. At present, many interpretations rely heavily on conceptual qualifications or theological emphases that do not appear or seem to fit well within Hebrews 6, or in some cases even within the book of Hebrews as a whole. By contrast, a more satisfying approach requires a closer reading of the text that facilitates interpreting the matter of impossibility in a way that has a clearer relation to this sermon's own stated categories and way of thinking.

Against this background, the chapters that follow will seek a substantively new way forward. We will begin with a close look at what exact kind of temptation the author says his audience is currently facing and what specific pastoral dynamics are created by that kind of temptation.

4

Not re-laying a foundation: the temptation to start over again

In an effort to re-examine the topic of what problem or temptation the audience of Hebrews faces, an important set of evidence appears in a frequently overlooked and very little studied feature of Hebrews 6:1–2, namely the author's use of imagery about re-laying a foundation. In particular, as the author urges the audience to move ahead towards greater maturity, he also exhorts them not to take another specific course of action that he characterizes as re-laying a foundation, headlined by repentance (*mē palin themelion kataballomenoi metanoias*).

A neglected and misunderstood metaphor

Despite the high level of attention that certain aspects of Hebrews 6 and the other warning passages in Hebrews have always received from scholars, the imagery of foundation-laying in Hebrews 6:1 has been quite neglected and as a result has also been misunderstood by those who do comment on it. While literature on topics such as repentance is voluminous, scholarship about foundation-laying in general and in Hebrews 6:1 remains quite scant by comparison. One illustration of this difference appears in the well-known *Theological Dictionary of the New Testament* (*TDNT*), in which the article on *metanoeō* (repentance) and cognates runs to 33.5 pages and provides a helpful introduction to a variety of scholarly positions and literature on the topic. By contrast, the article on *themelios* (foundation) and cognates covers only two pages and cites almost no specialized literature.[1] Moreover,

---

[1] Behm and Würthwein 1964–76: 4: 975–1008; Schmidt 1964–76: 3: 63–64.

since the time of *TDNT* (originally published in German between 1933 and 1989), no significant studies seem to have filled this noticeable lacuna in scholarship, especially regarding the significance of the metaphor in Hebrews 6:1 itself. Not surprisingly, given the noticeable lack of attention given to the topic, commentaries and articles on Hebrews 6:1 have little to depend on when addressing the topic of foundation-laying and so devote little space to exploring its meaning, and also end up relying on some faulty assumptions about what this image connotes and how it fits within its immediate context.

Of particular note regarding faulty assumptions is the way in which most scholars take the notion of re-laying a foundation to be essentially synonymous with other concepts that appear in the preceding context of Hebrews, such as that of continuing too long with a milk-only diet throughout 5:12–14, still needing to be taught the 'rudiments of the beginning of the oracles of God' in 5:12, or leaving the 'word of the beginning of Christ' to go on to more advanced topics, mentioned in 6:1. When all these notions are simply equated with one another, as often happens, the exhortation not to 're-lay a foundation' is viewed merely as another way of stating that the audience should go beyond simpler, elementary aspects of Christian teaching to learn about more advanced topics. F. F. Bruce, for example, interprets along these lines: '"So," [the author] says, "let us stop discussing the rudiments; do not let us start laying our foundations all over again." The rudiments . . . and the foundation are the same thing described in two different figures.'[2] Likewise, Craig Koester equates the basics or rudiments and the foundation when he says that the author of Hebrews 'wants to move beyond the basics. He wants to build on the foundation rather than relaying it, and to stop reviewing the alphabet to proceed to the study of literary composition.'[3] To similar effect, Witherington observes: 'Most commentators assume that the list in Hebrews 6:1–2 refers to the subject matter of elementary Christian teaching, and there can be little doubt that this is correct'. Accordingly, he notes:

> Our author does not want his audience to forget what they learned at the earlier stages, for example, forgetting to repent when necessary;

[2] Bruce 1990: 138.

[3] Koester 2001: 304; cf. 300, 310.

> these things are foundational. Rather, he wants them to move along to more advanced subjects, building on top of the original elementary learning.[4]

When interpreted along these lines, the concern of the author of Hebrews about not re-laying a foundation is understood as a metaphor arising from within a pedagogical sphere of discourse, describing a need for the audience to advance beyond an early, more elementary stage of education to a more advanced one. As Thomas Schreiner says, not re-laying a foundation means that the audience should not keep rehearsing the basic doctrines of the faith 'over and over' but should instead stretch themselves with more difficult topics that will promote 'further growth'.[5]

However, despite how commonly this equation is made between milk, rudiments, word of beginning and foundation-laying,[6] the arguments used to support the equation have significant problems. Two examples especially help to illustrate how this is so.

First, Paul Ellingworth appeals to the syntax of Hebrews 6:1 in support of this common reading. In his assessment:

> The structure of the sentence suggests that vv. 1b–2, μὴ πάλιν θεμέλιον καταβαλλόμενοι [not laying again a foundation], express negatively what ἀφέντες τὸν τῆς ἀρχῆς τοῦ Χριστοῦ λόγον [leaving behind the word of the beginning of Christ] states positively. If so, the list which occupies the rest of vv. 1–2 specifies the content of the 'beginning of the word of Christ.'[7]

Yet this interpretation produces noticeable tensions with the text. For one thing, it requires saying that, after spending several verses, from 5:12 through most of 6:1, explaining why the audience should leave elementary things *behind* and move on to maturity, the author only then pauses

[4] Witherington 2007: 208, 209.

[5] Schreiner 2020: 174–175. Similarly, Peterson 2020: 149–150.

[6] Others who equate the 'foundation' with milk, rudiments and/or word of beginning include Owen 1956–57: 244; Adams 1967: 383; Solari 1970: 62; Michel 1975: 238 n. 4; Hughes 1977: 196; Attridge 1989: 163; Lane 1991: 140; Weiss 1991: 335–336; Ellingworth 1993: 311; deSilva 2000: 215; L. T. Johnson 2006: 153; Mitchell 2007: 122; Thompson 2008: 132; Moffitt 2011: 182–183; Boda 2015: 175; Healy 2016: 112; D. E. Johnson 2018: 80; Peterson 2020: 149; Schreiner 2020: 174–175; Cara 2024: 180–181, 187.

[7] Ellingworth 1993: 311.

to provide a fairly lengthy description of the elementary things that he wants the audience not to keep repeating. The logic of the author's argument therefore becomes fairly odd, since it makes his flow of thought work somewhat against his own stated exhortation. As Bruce summarizes: '"So," he says, "let us stop discussing the rudiments . . ." . . . Before he goes on, however, he lists some of the rudiments'.[8] More problematically, though, by equating 'the word of the beginning of Christ' with the list of beliefs and practices that follows in verses 1b–2, scholars bring into sharp juxtaposition how the list that follows actually has nothing specific to say about Christ or anything else that is distinctively Christian but could just as easily summarize core beliefs and practices of many non-Christian Jewish groups of that day, as many others have noted.[9] Indeed, the list in 6:1b–2 begins with repentance from dead works and faith in God and then continues with instructions about washings, laying on of hands, resurrection of the dead and eternal judgment. As Harold Attridge comments: 'It is striking how little in this summary is distinctive of Christianity', noting that it sounds more like 'a catalogue of Jewish catechesis'.[10] Similarly, Marie Isaacs says: 'As this list stands there is nothing specifically Christian about any of its items. All form part of Jewish faith and practice of the period.'[11] In fact, Bruce notes how the items in the list all 'belonged to the creed of a Pharisaic Jew' as well as to that 'of a nonconformist Jew of Essene or comparable outlook'.[12]

At a minimum, these initial observations should give us pause, prior to our simply equating the rudiments or word of the beginning of Christ with the items in the foundation list that follows – a foundation which the author says not to re-lay. We at least need to consider more carefully whether the word of the beginning of Christ and the not-specifically-Christian content of the foundation actually represent two different things.

Second, a more significant problem with interpretations that equate the foundational content in 6:1 with milk, rudiments and word of beginning

[8] Bruce 1990: 138. Cf. Koester 2001: 310: 'Despite chiding them for needing milk, he proceeds to give them solid food. At the same time, he does not refrain from the basics altogether' and instead goes on 'listing the teachings he is *not* going to review (6:1b–2)'; emphasis original.

[9] E.g. Adams 1967: 379; Witherington 2007: 209; Thompson 2008: 132–133; D. E. Johnson 2018: 80, 83; Schenck 2019: 18; Peterson 2020: 150.

[10] Attridge 1989: 163.

[11] Isaacs 1992: 28. See also L. T. Johnson 2006: 158.

[12] Bruce 1990: 139.

emerges in the justification that scholars sometimes give for making the equation, namely an appeal to how all of these images were supposed to be used synonymously in Greek discussions of childhood education. Most influential in this regard has been James Thompson's view in *The Beginnings of Christian Philosophy* that, 'All of these terms were used for the beginning of philosophical study' in Greek thought. 'In each instance, the author envisions a lower level of instruction which is taught and from which one passes to a higher level of instruction.'[13] Along similar lines, David deSilva (citing Thompson) says that the metaphor 'foundation' is 'a common expression for elementary education, especially in philosophical schools'.[14] On further investigation, though, the evidence that Thompson and deSilva appeal to in order to make this equation does not adequately demonstrate their conclusion but actually points in the opposite direction.

To be sure, when it comes to something like a milk diet, Thompson's and deSilva's claims are correct: the metaphor is often used in Greek pedagogical discussions to describe an early, temporary stage in education that is distinct from the later, more mature stages that are intended to follow.[15] Philo, for example, makes particularly frequent use of a milk–meat contrast in which milk can be identified with early, simpler stages of education in the encyclical sciences and meat stands for the more advanced study that a student moves on to thereafter, such as the study of philosophy (*Good Person* 160) or of virtue (*Prelim. Studies* 19). In such contexts, the diet of milk is not disparaged in itself; it is helpful and appropriate to an early stage of development. Yet the diet of meat is still better because it is 'perfect' (*teleiai* [*Agriculture* 9]) or 'more complete' for adult life (*teleioteras* [*Prelim. Studies* 19]).[16] In other words, milk is good for an infant largely because the infant is not able to handle something more substantive. But, especially given the well-roundedness that a milk diet lacks, that diet is still designed from the outset to be temporary. The

[13] Thompson 1982: 30.

[14] deSilva 2000: 216.

[15] See especially the references and explanation found in Attridge 1989: 158–162. Note as well that Attridge does not include foundation in his discussion of the pedagogical metaphors used by the author of Hebrews in this part of his letter. In personal conversation, Attridge confirmed that this omission is purposeful, since the foundation image is being used differently from the other metaphors that precede it. This decision to omit also fits with what will be shown below regarding key differences between the milk metaphor in Heb. 5 and the foundation metaphor as it is typically used elsewhere in Greek literature.

[16] Translations of Philo are cited from Yonge 1993.

problem with a milk diet emerges, then, when it is held on to for too long and a person does not move past it. Accordingly, Philo elsewhere associates reliance on milk with continuing immaturity, such as preoccupation with the pleasures of the senses, which an older person should move beyond in favour of being self-guided by the wisdom of Scripture (*Migration* 28–29). Epictetus too employs this image and in a similar way. Describing children as those preoccupied with amusement and the wise man as the one who studies law, he asks: 'Are you not willing, like children, to be weaned and to partake of more solid food?' (*Diss.* 2.16.39).[17] While milk stands for different specific things in different passages, then, it still consistently refers to something that is inherently incomplete, temporary and meant from the beginning to be replaced.[18]

Clearly, as scholars generally recognize, all of these characteristic features of a milk diet are exactly why the author of Hebrews also uses the milk metaphor and speaks of rudiments and the word of beginning in Hebrews 5:12 – 6:1a. While he concedes that his audience does presently need milk, which shows that the content of a milk diet is good as far as it goes (5:12), he also points out that their continued reliance on milk alone is not natural and insists that milk does not constitute a sufficient diet for the further maturation they need (5:14). He therefore announces his intention to leave discussion of basic or rudimentary topics behind in 6:1a[19] and urges his audience to move forward in their development to completeness or maturity in 6:1b. In all of these ways, the author's use of milk, rudiments and word of beginning fits quite closely with how other Greek authors generally used such images, describing an early, temporary stage of education which is good but incomplete and therefore must be moved past.

At the same time, though, while scholars have correctly interpreted the import of the milk, rudiments and beginning word in 5:12 – 6:1a,

---

[17] Translations of Epictetus are cited from Oldfather 1998.

[18] The milk metaphor can also be used in other ways in ancient literature. For survey and analysis, see Penniman 2017, esp. p. 203. However, the kinds of uses just cited seem to provide the best background for understanding the metaphor's use in Heb. 5:12–14, as is generally recognized.

[19] Michel (1975: 237), Ellingworth (1993: 311–312), Koester (2001: 303) and L. T. Johnson (2006: 158) all cite helpful evidence from Euripides, Plutarch and Epictetus showing that the participle 'leaving behind' is a simple transitional device in Greek rhetoric, indicating that the author has been talking about certain topics (evidently more elementary ones) before and now announces his intention to go on to focus on other ones (evidently more mature ones). This simple statement of intention to 'move on to something else' (Ellingworth 1993: 311) again makes it unlikely that the list in 6:1b–2 reverts to enumerating the prior 'elementary' topics.

the problem arises when they then seek to equate the foundation-laying metaphor with these others. Contrary to what is sometimes claimed, the evidence from Greek authors shows that foundation-laying imagery is characteristically *not* used for the same purposes as these others but rather for something that is conceptually quite opposite to them.

To unpack this, we must note how the evidence that Thompson and deSilva appeal to for grouping foundation-laying with these other images does not actually support their conclusion. Despite deSilva's claim that it is 'common' for Greek authors to use foundation imagery to refer to the early, temporary stages of education, both he and Thompson only cite one example where this use of foundation imagery is supposed to occur, namely Epictetus, *Dissertationes* 2.15.8.[20] On further analysis, though, their appeal to that example in fact seems to be misplaced. In that passage, Epictetus does not actually describe earlier and later stages of educational development. He instead gives advice about human decision-making and the circumstances in which a person should remain doggedly steadfast in a decision previously made rather than changing his or her mind. On that topic, Epictetus notes how one's degree of determination not to change one's mind about an earlier decision should really depend on whether the decision in question was a sound one to begin with or not. He asks:

> Do you not wish to make your beginning and your foundation firm, that is, to consider whether your decision is sound or unsound, and only after you have done that proceed to rear thereon the structure of your determination and your firm resolve?

Evidently, this passage is not actually talking about stages of education, and is also not describing a movement from earlier to later stages of learning, such that one should leave the first stage behind for the second. Rather, the foundation it describes is actually something that a person would hope *not* to leave behind, since their original decision was well founded from the start. This usage of foundation-laying imagery is therefore quite different from what was seen above regarding milk or other educational imagery.

So, then, the reasons that scholars have cited for equating the

[20] Note that it appears to be incorrectly cited by Thompson as *Diss.* 2.15.18 (1982: 30 n. 52) but is later correctly cited by deSilva as *Diss.* 2.15.8 (2000: 216 n. 10).

'foundation' in Hebrews 6:1 with milk, rudiments or beginning word are not particularly well formed or persuasive. To the contrary, some of the main evidence cited in support of that equation actually calls it into question. These initial observations therefore show the need for more careful investigation of foundation-laying imagery itself in order to gain a greater understanding of how this metaphor is often used in Greek literature, as a point of comparison for revisiting Hebrews 6:1–2.

Key characteristics of foundation-laying in the ancient world

We move now to take a broader look at relevant evidence from ancient Greek discussions of foundations and the accompanying use of foundation-laying imagery, especially as this compares to the use of metaphors like that of a milk diet, mentioned above.[21] In so doing, three characteristics of foundations especially stand out as crucial for understanding how the metaphor of foundation-laying is commonly used, and these will help to illuminate important aspects of its use in Hebrews 6 as well.

First, in ancient Greek literature one of the most defining characteristics of a foundation is not its purposefully temporary nature, as is the case with a milk diet, but its permanence instead. When describing literal buildings, Josephus notes how Solomon selected 'strong stones' (*lithōn ischthras*) for the foundations (*themelious*) of the temple 'and such as would resist the force of time: these were to . . . become a basis and a sure foundation for that superstructure which was erected over it' (*Ant.* 8.63).[22] Here the constant and abiding nature of the foundation is what provides longevity for the temple as a whole. Similarly, when foundation imagery is used metaphorically, Philo says that the role of virtues within a person is to secure 'a firm and strong foundation for a lasting building' (*Cherubim* 103). As seen above, Epictetus also uses the imagery this way regarding decision-making, saying that a person's first decision must lay a foundation on which to build '[their] determination and [their] firm resolve' (*Diss.* 2.15.8). In biblical usage too, LXX Psalm 103:8 says that God

[21] The milk metaphor is clearly the most prominent of the descriptions in this portion of Hebrews, compared to rudiments or word of beginning, since it is introduced first in 5:12 and is used in a more sustained way than the others (vv. 12–14). Accordingly, that metaphor will serve as a focal point in what follows for the sake of comparison and contrast with foundation-laying.

[22] Translations of Josephus are cited from Whiston 1895.

'establishes the earth on her sure foundation: it shall not be moved for ever', and it is commonplace in Scripture to explain the enduring nature of things such as the earth (LXX Prov. 3:19; 8:29), mountains (LXX Ps. 103:8), heavenly bodies (LXX Ps. 8:4), a palace (LXX Prov. 18:19), the city of God (on earth [LXX Pss 47:9; 86:1, 5; 103:5; Isa. 44:28] or in heaven [Heb. 11:10; Rev. 21:14, 19]) or the temple (LXX Ps. 77:69) on the basis of their having foundations. Similarly, the certainty of wisdom (LXX Prov. 8:23) and of God's testimonies (LXX Ps. 118:152; cf. 2 Tim. 2:19) is due to their foundations; eternal treasure provides a sure foundation because it lasts for ever, unlike earthly wealth (1 Tim. 6:19); and a person who is rightly related to God is like a well-founded house that lasts (Luke 6:48–49). In fact, so closely are foundations associated with steadfastness or permanence that the former becomes a ready-made shorthand for the latter when New Testament authors describe believers as 'rooted and founded' (Eph. 3:17), 'founded and firm' (Col. 1:23), or 'confirmed, strengthened, and founded' (1 Pet. 5:10).

Of course, the permanence that a foundation provides is due to the fact that a foundation is not discarded or moved on from but remains continually present in the building structure itself. With this in mind, Philo describes the enjoyment of pleasure as the foundation of all other human passions:

> Because it is almost at the bottom of them all, as a sort of base or foundation [*tis archē kai themelios*] for them, for desire *originates* in the love of pleasure, and pain *consists* in the removal of pleasure; and fear again is *caused* by a desire to guard against its absence. So it is plain that all the passions are *anchored* on pleasure; and perhaps one might say that they would absolutely have had no existence at all if pleasure had not been previously laid down as *a foundation to support* them.
> (*Alleg. Interp.* 3.113; emphasis added)

Here, as elsewhere, a foundation is viewed as the abiding condition, even the *continually present source or cause*, for the thing that is built on it. However, the same clearly cannot be said of a milk diet, which is instead meant to be used for a time and then left behind. Similarly, elsewhere Philo describes how, 'like a foundation, the sense of taste is the *cause of duration* of animals' since it constantly influences them to eat (*Alleg.*

Interp. 2.96; emphasis added). Or again, virtue plays the role of 'a firm and strong foundation' for a person's character, making him or her 'a lasting building' through its continual influence, so that nothing else can come along to 'separate and alienate the soul from honesty' (*Cherubim* 103).

For this reason, ancient writers frequently pair foundation imagery with imagery about fountains, which constantly supply water, or about roots, which provide continuing support and sustenance to a tree. For example, 'everything which the external senses suffer, it endures not without the support of the mind; for the mind is *its fountain, and the foundation* [*themelios*] *on which it is supported*' (*Alleg. Interp.* 2.41; emphasis added). Or again, nature functions as 'the fountain, and root, and foundation of all arts and science', because it provides 'the oldest of principles . . . upon which all speculations are built up' (*Heir* 116; see also *Creation* 41; *Sacrifices* 25; *Prelim. Studies* 146; *Virtues* 158; Eph. 3:17).

Crucially, then, a foundation is defined by its constant and abiding presence in the building, which imparts stability and longevity to the whole structure, and therefore becomes virtually synonymous with permanence itself. For these same reasons, a foundation is clearly also meant to be laid *once for all* and to remain entirely fixed after that.[23]

This again helps to point out how different the implications of re-laying a foundation are compared to prolonging a milk diet. While both are actions which the author of Hebrews urges the audience against taking in 5:12 – 6:2, nevertheless each action entails something quite different. Prolonging a milk diet is problematic because it entails remaining in a state of immaturity, when someone should move forward to maturity. By contrast, re-laying a foundation is retrogressive and entails saying that something is so fundamentally wrong with an existing building, all the way down to the bottom, that the whole thing must be entirely dismantled. *Put differently, prolonging a milk diet means keeping something in place that is intended to be temporary, but re-laying a foundation means uprooting something that is intended to be permanent and instead dismantling what already exists to start all over again from the ground up.* In this sense, the idea of re-laying a foundation in Hebrews 6:1b brings

[23] As Hughes (1977: 196) correctly notes: 'A *foundation* is something that is either there or not there . . . Consequently, there can be no question of *laying* [it] *again*'; emphasis original. Similarly, Cara (2024: 187) writes: 'One does not abandon the foundation when constructing the remainder of the house, but builds upon it. However, to lay again a foundation is improper, a house only needs one foundation.'

up a radically different course of action from what had previously been mentioned in 5:12 – 6:1a.[24]

Second, not only are foundations laid once for all and are therefore synonymous with permanence in Greek literature, but they also play a normative, essence-defining role for the buildings that are erected upon them. In fact, the entire character of a given building is often thought to be contained within and continually determined by the ingredients present in its foundation, which further underscores how radical the notion of re-laying a foundation actually is.

With regard to literal buildings, the size and quality of a foundation play a crucial role in determining the shape, potential height and overall quality of the superstructure to be built upon it. Josephus therefore notes how the size and quality of the stones that Solomon used for the temple's foundation were necessary

> in order to sustain with ease the vast superstructures, and precious ornaments, whose own weight was to be not less than the weight of those other high and heavy buildings, which the king designed to be very ornamental and magnificent.
> (*Ant.* 8.63)

In this way, the foundation helps to determine the building's essential character, including what is both fitting and possible to use in its superstructure. In fact, Herod the Great evidently added 20 cubits (9 m [30 ft]) to the height of the temple, but this proved to be too much for the foundations to hold and these new additions eventually collapsed (*Ant.* 15.391).

Similarly with metaphorical buildings, foundations help to define and determine the nature of what is built upon them. As a result, an important key to correctly understanding the nature of any structure consists

[24] Unfortunately, the particularity of the author's language about *not re-laying* a foundation is sometimes obscured from view in scholarly discourse and replaced with the positive sentiment that the audience *should build* on their existing foundation. Lane, for example (1991: 140), says: 'The writer is not asking the community to discard one aspect of Christian instruction for another but to build upon the solid foundation already laid for them.' Similarly, Witherington (2007: 208) states: 'Our author does not want his audience to forget what they learned at the earlier stages, for example, forgetting to repent when necessary; these things are foundational. Rather, he wants them to move along to more advanced subjects, building on top of the original elementary learning.' Such interpretative summaries replace the author's own negative language about what not to do, leaving only positive language about what to do.

in correctly identifying what its foundational elements are. Philo, for example, helps to define human nature by identifying its foundation. He maintains that it is the rational part of the soul that is human nature's oldest, foundational element [*themeliou tropon*] and therefore also its 'dominant' or most defining part (*Alleg. Interp.* 2.6). Similarly, knowledge of creation's founding is a prerequisite for properly understanding its nature (Philo, *Drunkenness* 31; cf. Job 38:4; Prov. 8:23; *1 Enoch* 15:9). Accordingly, when reading Scripture, Philo says that interpreters must first lay down certain truths 'by way of foundation; and on this foundation . . . raise up the rest of the [interpretative] building, following the rules of that wise architect [*architektonos*], allegory' (*Dreams* 2.8). Again, in the sciences, first principles delivered by philosophy act as 'roots and foundations' from which later, scientific deductions then 'appear to arise' (*Prelim. Studies* 146). Or again, in ethics, when Moses gave the Law, he first laid down 'principles as a kind of foundation of gentleness and humanity', which then determined the nature of individual legal provisions subsequently built upon those principles, such as laws about sabbatical years (*Alleg. Interp.* 2.110). Also, with regard to human character, the person who has 'first of all laid down temperance as a sort of foundation for the soul to rest upon' will then 'proceed to build up other virtues on this foundation' (*Contempl. Life* 34). However, if 'wickedness and passion are the foundations' of a person's character, he or she will act in accordance with it as well (*Sacrifices* 81; cf. *Giants* 30).

Clearly, then, foundation-laying is not just one passing stage in a building's growth, to move beyond later, but something uniquely determinative for every stage thereafter. In fact, a foundation defines the enduring nature of a structure as a whole, which certainly cannot be said for something like a milk diet.

It is also for this reason that the foundation of a building can even stand representatively for the building itself. Philo, for example, explains that when Moses describes the priests washing their belly, he refers to them washing something foundational to their persons, which therefore stands representatively for the need to wash the whole person:

> [W]e ought not to be ignorant that Moses repudiates the whole of the belly [by] giving a lively representation of the *whole from one part* . . . The filling of the belly is a most enduring and universal thing; and, as it were, a kind of *foundation* of the other passions

> [*themelios tis tōn allōn pathōn*]. At all events, there is not one of them which can find any existence if it is not *supported by* the belly, on which nature has made everything to depend.
> (*Alleg. Interp.* 3.145; emphasis added)

The belly, as foundation, represents the larger whole because it contains what essentially epitomizes or defines it. For similar reasons, ancient authors also affirm that a structure has been truly destroyed only if it is destroyed down 'to the very foundations' (Josephus, *Ant.* 4.310; cf. Deut. 32:22; Job 22:16; LXX Ps. 136:7; Josephus, *Ant.* 1.77; 5.31; Philo, *Moses* 2.157; *Rewards* 150; *Embassy* 132). Otherwise, the most crucial part of the edifice still remains.

Importantly, these characteristics of foundations also impact the way in which ancient authors use foundation imagery when discussing phases of education in particular. For example, while Philo may call the first stages of encyclical instruction 'milk', as discussed previously, he does not call them a 'foundation', precisely because these stages are purposefully only temporary – something to move past. He instead identifies the 'foundation' in education with something more basic and permanently present throughout the educational process, something which precedes encyclical instruction and remains constant throughout all subsequent stages of learning. Thus, describing a person as a house, he says:

> that the house may be firm and beautiful, let a good disposition and knowledge be laid as its foundations [*themelioi*], and on these foundations let virtues be built up in union with good actions, and let the ornaments of the front be the due comprehension of the encyclical branches of elementary instruction.
> (*Cherubim* 101)

So, then, early encyclical instruction is actually the third stage of education in this description and is built upon the foundation of one's personal disposition, which provides stability throughout all stages of learning (ibid. 102). Similarly, elsewhere Philo says:

> All the lessons and all the admonitions of instruction are built up and established on the nature which is calculated to receive instruction, as on a foundation previously laid [*themeliō prokatabeblēmenō*]; but

> if there is no natural foundation previously in existence, everything is useless.
> (*Names* 211)

Here again the foundation is not one temporary stage of education, to be replaced by another later on, but a person's enduring nature, which continually supports and helps to define every phase that follows. On the same note, Philo asks:

> Is not nature the fountain, and root, and foundation of all arts and sciences, or any other name you please to give the oldest of principles, nature, upon which all speculations are built up? And if nature be not first laid as the foundation, everything is imperfect [*atelē*].
> (*Heir* 116)

So, then, within discourse about education, foundation-laying imagery clearly has different connotations from those of milk-diet imagery, precisely because only the former describes something constant that has a continually normative and defining role in all that follows.

This again suggests that the foundation metaphor in Hebrews 6:1b is not at all interchangeable with the other metaphors used previously in 5:12 – 6:1a. Rather than describing something inherently limited and insufficient in its content that, by design, needs to be moved on from (as with a milk diet), foundations instead identify the abiding essence of a building that is clearly *not* to be left behind so long as a given building is to be kept at all. Simply put, *one does not re-lay a foundation unless something about an existing building and its foundation is so flawed that the whole thing needs to be dismantled and something else rebuilt in its place with an essentially different character*. In this sense, the notion of re-laying a foundation clearly does not equate to rehearsing the less complex elements of Christian instruction for too long, as some have supposed. This latter idea would be akin to regularly making necessary repairs to the walls of a building or some other part of its superstructure. By contrast, re-laying a foundation implies starting all over from the ground up in order to build something else of an essentially different kind in its place.

Third, another important characteristic of ancient thought about foundations is how foundations functioned as the grounds for a person's *confidence* in a building. For example, LXX Isaiah 28:16 says: 'Behold, I will lay for the foundations of Zion a stone, a costly, chosen, precious cornerstone for its foundations [*ta themelia*]; and the one who believes on it will certainly not be put to shame.' Similarly, in LXX Isaiah 14:32, 'The Lord has founded Zion, and through it the humble among the people will be saved' (cf. LXX Ps. 86:5). In the New Testament as well, good foundations give certainty of salvation and rewards (e.g. Matt. 7:21, 24–26; Rom. 9:33; 1 Tim. 6:19; 2 Tim. 2:19; 1 Pet. 2:6). In fact, even in Hebrews itself, certainty about the blessing to be obtained in the heavenly city derives from the kind of foundation (*tous themelious*) that the city has, namely one laid by its architect (*technitēs*), God (11:10; cf. Rev. 21:14, 19).

By implication, to consider re-laying a building's foundation clearly shows a fundamental *lack* of confidence in the building as a whole, not just with regard to its superstructure but all the way down to the bottom. In other words, re-laying a foundation would say that one has so little confidence in the building one inhabits that it seems necessary to dismantle and rebuild something with essentially different, stronger, more confidence-inducing materials in its place.

It is also important to note in this connection how the author of Hebrews himself melds rhetoric about house structures and confidence at various points in his letter. Early on, in 3:1–6, the author describes the house of God (vv. 2, 5, 6) of which Christ is the builder (v. 3) and over which he is son (v. 6), and he says that the members of his audience are part of that house *if* they hold on to their *confidence* firmly to the end (v. 14). Then later, in Hebrews 10, he reasons similarly that since Jesus is the great high priest over God's house (v. 21), the audience should have full assurance (v. 22) and therefore hold fast to their Christian confession (v. 23). It seems clear, then, that the author wants the house in which the audience currently dwells to be something in which they have great, continuing confidence so that they will remain in it patiently and with endurance. Yet the opposite course of action is also mentioned, in which the audience might instead abandon their present confidence (10:35–36) or fall away from what they currently profess (3:12; cf. 6:6), all of which the author warns them not to do.

Within the larger context of this rhetoric about confidence, then, the exhortation not to throw away existing confidence (10:35) and not to re-lay a foundation (6:1) are essentially the same. In this respect, the notion of re-laying a foundation ought not to be something the audience would even consider doing. In actual fact, though, Hebrews 6:1 shows that the audience is considering it, since the author strongly exhorts them not to do it.

On balance, then, the evidence above clearly shows that the foundation-laying metaphor must be distinguished from the milk diet and equivalent metaphors used earlier in 5:12 – 6:1a. Unlike these other images, re-laying a foundation does not refer to prolonging elementary things that are purposefully temporary and inherently incomplete. It instead describes abandoning what is most essential and enduring, something meant to be permanent, essence-defining and a source of abiding confidence. (See Table 4.1.)

Table 4.1 Key contrasts between foundation-laying and milk-diet imagery

Foundation	Intended to be permanent	Defines a building's essence	Source of strength and confidence	Desire to change it is problematic
Milk diet	Purposefully temporary	Limited content lacks important nutrients	Only appropriate to a period of immaturity	Unwillingness to change it is problematic

Tracing the flow of the author's deliberative rhetoric

Recognizing the key differences inherent within the two sets of metaphors used by the author of Hebrews casts the author's progression of thought in 5:11 – 6:2 in a particular light. This is important to grasp, as it also has implications for understanding the audience's situation, the choice the author sees them facing and therefore the force of his deliberative rhetoric.

Stepping back to look at the surrounding context, it is clear that Hebrews 5:11 – 6:12 covers a lot of hortatory ground, since it moves from concern that the audience is presently immature and still needs milk (5:11–14) to concern with much more severe topics such as rejecting the Son of God (6:6), destruction (6:8), and not experiencing salvation (6:9) or the ultimate inheritance of promises (6:12). When analysing the flow of thought in this section, it is important to make some clear distinctions.

Surely, being immature in faith and having a childish milk-diet are problematic in the author's estimation, since immaturity is associated with being unskilled in the word (5:13) and lacking the discernment that comes with a meat diet (5:14). By implication, remaining immature clearly increases the audience's spiritual risk and is something the author wishes to see changed by helping his readers to be ready for meat. Nevertheless, a milk diet does not produce destruction in itself. In that sense, for all its problems, having a milk diet is not the complete opposite of having a meat diet, because both milk-eaters and meat-eaters are still Christians receiving spiritual nutrition, as the author understands it. In other words, these two diets, while contrasting with each other *by degree*, are nevertheless on a continuum with each other, and neither one produces the destruction that the author describes later. In that respect, the prolongation of a milk diet is not the author's ultimate or deepest concern. In fact, the author does not reject milk but acknowledges that, at present, the audience does in fact *need* milk (5:12). Instead, from a rhetorical point of view, the complete opposite course of action from advancing to maturity – the course of action that the author directly opposes, which would produce destruction – does not consist in continuing to drink milk but in something else. This, it seems, is why the author shifts in 6:1b to using a different kind of analogy from the others he has already introduced, in order to describe, not the relative inadequacy of prolonging a milk diet or repeating mere rudimentary topics of instruction, which results in *inadequate* growth, but instead the much more destructive scenario of the audience's dismantling altogether the house they currently live in, down to its foundations, in order to start over again in a fundamentally different way.

This, then, is how Hebrews 6:1 helps to advance the author's rhetoric beyond what he said in 5:11–14, by opening up the fuller scope of the deliberative contrast he has already adumbrated previously in the letter (e.g. 2:1–4; 3:6, 12–14; 4:1, 11, 14–16), not just about the problem of immaturity but about the greater problem of apostasy and destruction. Since the members of the audience are presently immature and thereby in a position of increased spiritual risk, they need to go on to maturity through the meaty instruction which the author will give them in this sermon.

Be that as it may, the author also recognizes that going forward to maturity will be difficult for the audience, especially due to their present state of being dull of hearing (5:11) and sluggish (6:12). To the contrary, what they are tempted to do instead, and what the author directly exhorts them against doing in 6:1b–2, is to go further *backward*, dismantling their present house and starting entirely over in a different way.

Viewed like this, Hebrews 6:1 describes a fork in the road that is crucial to understand – a clear deliberative contrast between entirely opposite courses of action. *One path leads from present immaturity forward to greater maturity (going from milk to meat), and the other leads from present immaturity backward to an abandonment of the entire spiritual house that the audience presently inhabits (i.e. their profession of Christ) in favour of something essentially different.* (See Table 4.2.)

Table 4.2 Fork in the road: the audience's condition and the two opposite paths they face

The audience's present condition	*What they are presently tempted to do*	*What they ought to do instead*
Sluggish of hearing (5:11; 6:12), immature (5:12–13), unskilled in the word of righteousness (5:13)	Re-lay an old foundation (6:1b–2)	Go forward to maturity (6:1), through instruction about Christ as Melchizedekian high priest (5:10–11)

It should be noted at this juncture, though, that most scholars have not understood Hebrews 6:1 in this way. In particular, the reading described above takes the main verb in 6:1 (a hortatory subjunctive, *pherōmetha*) to articulate a positive exhortation about the direction the audience *should* go in and then takes the negative participial clause that follows (*mē . . . kataballomenoi*) to be describing an *opposite* direction in which the audience should *not* go. By contrast, most scholars have taken the participial clause in question to be synonymous with or epexegetical of the main verb, essentially expressing some aspect of how it is that the audience should go on to maturity, namely by not just repeating elementary instruction. However, this synonymous reading fails to account properly for the radical nature of what re-laying a foundation entails compared to prolonging a milk diet, as has been explained above. Moreover, it also overlooks how the author of Hebrews constructs his deliberative rhetoric elsewhere in the sermon where he articulates two opposite courses of action using the same syntactical construction found in 6:1.

Of special note here is the very similar hortatory context in 10:24–25, where the author again uses a hortatory subjunctive regarding what the audience *should* do, followed by a participial clause describing what they should *not* do. Yet the meaning of the participial clause is not synonymous with the main verb; it instead builds a complete contrast to it that is about not abandoning the Christian faith entirely. Specifically, the hortatory subjunctive in 10:24 urges the audience ('Let us consider' [*katanoōmen*]) to excite one another to love and good deeds, which is something crucial to do for the sake of continuing forward in their Christian profession. Then this positive exhortation is followed by a negative participial phrase, 'not leaving behind the assembling of yourselves together' (*mē enkataleipontes*) in 10:25. Therefore, not only is the syntactical construction in 10:24–25 the same as in 6:1, but also the content being described is essentially the same. After all, the participial phrase in 10:25 exhorts the audience against abandoning the Christian assembly, and in context this is part of the author's exhortation regarding how to hold fast their confession of Christ as high priest (10:22–23), rather than sinning wilfully after receiving knowledge of the truth (10:26), which would amount to spurning the Son of God and outraging the Spirit of grace, thus bringing a consequent expectation of judgment (10:29). In this way, 10:24–25 are clearly describing the same basic deliberative contrast between two completely opposite courses of action as are seen in 6:1. In both places, the hortatory subjunctive and the participial phrase lay out two diametrically opposite courses with opposite results, one involving perseverance forward in Christian hope and the other involving its abandonment.

This comparison to Hebrews 10:24–25 therefore helps to show how natural it is, within this author's own style of writing, to read Hebrews 6:1 as describing a crucial crossroads faced by the letter's audience. Reading 6:1 in this way also helps to account for the author's move from talking about mere immaturity in 5:12–14 to talking instead about the risk of destruction in Hebrews 6. Recognizing the audience's presently immature state of contenting themselves only with milk, rudiments or beginning words, the author lays out two possibilities going forward – one that is life-giving and the other destructive – and urges them to take the proper course.

In the light of this, it also becomes clear that, contrary to what revisionist scholars have suggested, the text of Hebrews does not *only* urge its audience to go *forward*, positively speaking. It also describes a temptation for them to go *backward*, which it urges them not to do. This means that the idea of the audience's being tempted to go backward is not a matter of mere inference from the theological sections of Hebrews, much less a mere product of traditional scholars' assumptions or biases being read into the text. It is instead something that is directly described by the author himself and specifically in his exhortations to his own audience – precisely the part of Hebrews' rhetoric that revisionist scholars have said is most determinative for understanding the original audience's situation. In this way, a key aspect of traditional scholarship on Hebrews is shown to have been correct, even if for reasons that are different from those which scholars have traditionally appealed to in support of it.

Yet the question arises: what specifically is the audience tempted to go back to and why? Answering this requires looking more closely at the larger context in 6:1–6 in order to observe more detail about the foundation that the audience is told not to re-lay and precisely why the author believes it is inadequate. This will shed additional light on the audience's exact situation, the precise nature of the choice that they face, and why the author feels it necessary to exhort them in just the way that he does, not only in 6:1–6 but throughout the letter as a whole.

5

Once having been enlightened: a decisive transition forward

In the preceding chapter, we have seen how re-laying a foundation is quite a radical notion that involves people starting over again from the ground up and therefore implies that something is so fundamentally wrong with an existing building that an essentially different structure (i.e. one with a different foundation) is needed in its place. Yet if starting over with a different foundation is what the author of Hebrews must urge his audience not to do with respect to the spiritual house they presently inhabit, it becomes important to understand the precise nature of the alternative foundation that the author warns them not to re-lay, what exactly defines its composition, why the audience is considering re-laying it and why the author urgently wants them not to do so. All of this requires giving further attention to Hebrews 6:1–2 itself and to various aspects of the larger context that help to illuminate the meaning and significance of this important exhortation.

The search for context: two closely connected lists

While there are many factors that must be considered when seeking to understand the alternative foundation and the list of items that comprise its content in Hebrews 6:1b–2, one particularly important feature in the immediate context is the presence of another list of religious experiences in 6:4–5, which will be explored in detail below. In that second list, the author describes a second set of religious experiences, namely having once been enlightened, having tasted the heavenly gift, having partaken of

Table 5.1 The two lists in Hebrews 6:1–6

6:1b–2	Repentance from dead works	Faith in God	Instruction in washings	Laying on of hands	Resurrection of the dead	Eternal judgment
6:4–5	Once having been enlightened	Tasted the heavenly gift	Shared the Holy Spirit	Tasted the good word of God	. . . and the powers of the coming age	

the Holy Spirit, and having tasted the good word of God and the powers of the age to come.[1]

When comparing these two lists with each other (see Table 5.1), even in a prima facie way, several observations suggest that the content and significance of each is meant to be understood in comparison and contrast to the other. Not only are both lists of similar size and found in close proximity to each other, but they also have important thematic connections. Of particular note is how the two lists are closely connected to the first two (out of a total of three) instances of the word *metanoia* (repentance) found in Hebrews. Interestingly, though, while the topic of repentance connects the two lists, it also stands in a diametrically opposite relationship to each list. In the former list, repentance is the first thing mentioned, thereby headlining the foundation described there. By contrast, in the subsequent list, repentance is not a part of the list but is instead what a person cannot be restored to after experiencing the items mentioned in the second list and then falling away, as 6:6 states. These and other factors therefore suggest that the two lists are related to each other in the author's argument and should be looked at in close connection to each other. Doing so will provide an important next step in understanding the nature and significance of the foundation that 6:1 says should not be laid again.

However, even while noting this connection between the two lists in 6:1b–2 and 6:4–5, many other questions about interpreting each list remain. Of particular note has been the debate about discerning the conceptual background for each list, since knowing this would help to explain the items in each, and their significance. After all, most of the individual

[1] Technically, the list continues into 6:6 with the statement that the people under consideration have also 'fallen away', but this additional participle effects a clear shift in focus to describe something negative that occurs despite the positive benefits first described in 6:4–5. The exact meaning of this additional participial phrase will therefore be considered later.

items that appear in both lists are spoken of quite commonly within at least some Christian teaching found elsewhere in the New Testament, as well as in various strains of non-Christian Jewish thought and sometimes even in broader Greco-Roman religious and philosophical thought. As a result, scholars have made various proposals for establishing the background to each list and how to understand their overall composition.

One example of the tensions involved here appears when considering the composition of the list in 6:1b–2 as a whole. The starting point for most scholars has been to assume that this list summarizes the content of the elementary Christian instruction or milk that the author of Hebrews wants the audience to leave behind.[2] Of course, it has been shown above that this assumption goes against the very nature of the foundation metaphor. Even apart from that consideration, though, this common scholarly assumption also produces other tensions. This is evident when those assuming that the list in 6:1b–2 summarizes elementary Christian instruction then also note with puzzlement that nothing in the list is distinctively Christian. As mentioned before, Harold Attridge states: 'It is striking how little in this summary is distinctive of Christianity . . . Most conspicuously absent is any explicit christological affirmation.'[3] Similarly, Marie Isaacs notes: 'As this list [in 6:1b–2] stands there is nothing specifically Christian about any of its items. All form part of Jewish faith and practice of the period.'[4] In fact, F. F. Bruce even observes that all the components in this list 'are consistent with Judaism' and 'belonged to the creed of a Pharisaic Jew' as well as that 'of a nonconformist Jew of Essene or comparable outlook.'[5] The content of 6:1b–2, taken as a whole, therefore seems quizzical, which raises questions about the proper way to understand it.

In addition, the tensions that scholars experience with the two lists in Hebrews 6:1–6 can also be illustrated when considering not only the first

[2] The observation that this is the common assumption among scholars is also made by Adams (1967: 378); Weeks (1976: 75); and Witherington (2007: 209). For examples of those interpreting 6:1b–2 as just described, see Solari 1970: 60; Isaacs 1992: 28; deSilva 2000: 216; Stedman 2009: 69; D. E. Johnson 2018: 80, 82; Peterson 2020: 149; Schreiner 2020: 171; Grindheim 2023: 304–305; Cara 2024: 186, 188–190.

[3] Attridge 1989: 163–164. Cf. Owen 1956–57: 244; Adams 1967: 379; Solari 1970: 60; Weeks 1976: 76; Weiss 1991: 336, who says these items are lacking in Christological content and 'somit eher in den Raum des Judentums als in den des Christentums verweisen'; Peterson 2020: 149.

[4] Isaacs 1992: 28.

[5] Bruce 1990: 139.

list as a whole but also individual components within it. After all, many items in that list, most notably washings and laying on of hands, were practised so widely in some form or another in the ancient world as to be nearly ubiquitous, not only among Christians and non-Christian Jews but in parts of the broader pagan world as well.[6] In theory, then, quite a wide range of specific referents could potentially be in view when considering individual items.

In order to narrow things down further, scholars have therefore appealed to various possible background contexts as the key to understanding each of the lists in 6:1b–2 and 6:4–5. This includes appeal to the experience of the wilderness generation of Israel,[7] the content of the Levitical codes of the Old Testament,[8] aspects of Second Temple Jewish belief and practice in general,[9] the preaching of Jesus in particular,[10] or the practice of the earliest apostolic church reflected in Acts and elsewhere as the crucial background for defining both the list in 6:1b–2 and its counterpart in 6:4–5.[11] Yet choices between such a wide array of possible conceptual backgrounds also precipitate wide swings in interpretative conclusions,[12] which then poses difficult questions about how to know which is appropriate to Hebrews 6 itself. For example, by surveying various possible background contexts, some have been led to argue that 'instruction in washings' in Hebrews 6:2 refers to instruction about Jewish proselyte baptism, John the Baptist's baptism, ceremonial washings in other Jewish sects, Christian baptism, and how they all differed from one

[6] For a survey of some possibilities, see e.g. Hughes 1977: 199–202; Ellingworth 1993: 315–316.

[7] Weeks 1976: 78; Mathewson 1999: 222–225; Gleason 2007: 352f.

[8] Wuest 1962: 51; Bruce 1990: 141.

[9] Attridge 1989: 164–165; Bruce 1990: 139–141; Emmrich 2003: 83; L. T. Johnson 2006: 158; Witherington 2007: 209–210; Thompson 2008: 132–133. Moreover, these scholars appeal to quite a wide range of specific possible backgrounds within Second Temple Judaism, including the thought and practice of the Pharisees, Essenes, the Qumran community, Jewish washing rituals in general and (in Emmrich's case) Second Temple 'retributive pneumatological traditions' in general.

[10] Adams 1967: 381; Thompson 1982: 30–31; Witherington 2007: 209.

[11] Ellingworth 1993: 316; deSilva 2000: 218; Koester 2001: 305; Mitchell 2007: 120, 129; Moffitt 2011: 184; Schreiner 2020: 177. To a lesser extent, consideration is also given at times to possible connections to the Greco-Roman mystery religions and the later baptismal practices of the post-apostolic church (e.g. Hughes 1977: 199–202; Lane 1991: 141; Ellingworth 1993: 315, 320), though these have not been considered to be as decisive.

[12] If, for example, the content of both lists is specifically describing the wilderness experience of Israel, then neither list is directly describing Christian experience. By contrast, if washings and laying on of hands refer directly to Christian baptism and anointing with the Spirit as described in Acts, then the exact opposite is true.

another.[13] Yet such an omnibus reading requires importing quite a lot of detailed information into Hebrews 6, despite the fact that there is no clear reference to at least most of the washings just mentioned within Hebrews itself, nor any clear use of the sort of conceptual distinctions that would be needed to identify all of these washings and to distinguish some of them from others. This interpretation therefore has great potential to be foisting foreign considerations upon Hebrews without clear justification for doing so.

When considering the two lists in Hebrews 6:1–6, then, past scholarship has experienced significant difficulties in making clear sense of their construction. As a result, it becomes methodologically important to prioritize the interpretative context that is supplied within the thought-world of Hebrews itself whenever possible, to see what clues its pages provide about the meaning of the individual terms in each list and how each list fits together to form a coherent whole.

With that goal in mind, we will proceed below to look at the second list first, since its interpretation has generally proven less vexing. This will then provide a clearer point of departure in the next chapter for looking more closely at the first one by comparison.

Transition into and experience of the new covenant

The list that is found in Hebrews 6:4–5 begins with a reference to 'once having been enlightened' (*hapax phōtisthentas*). While the term 'enlightenment' can mean different things in different contexts, in Hebrews it has specific connotations that are crucial for understanding the entire list that follows.

All told, the verb *phōtizō* only occurs twice in Hebrews, once in 6:4 and again in 10:32, but in the latter verse it clearly describes the starting point of the audience's new-covenant-specific faith and experience. In a poignant context that provides important information about the audience's history, the author reflects in 10:32–34 on the early days of this group's existence and describes how, after the audience was enlightened

[13] See Solari 1970: 67; Michel 1975: 239; Hughes 1977: 201–202; Weiss 1991: 339; Ellingworth 1993: 315; Koester 2001: 305; L. T. Johnson 2006: 159; Witherington 2007: 210; Healy 2016: 117; Schreiner 2020: 176; Grindheim 2023: 307; Cara 2024: 189–190.

(*phōtisthentes*), they had great joy despite also facing serious persecution. Importantly, evidence throughout the letter helps to confirm how the origins of the group are to be traced back to their having heard about, believed in and experienced the benefits of a Christian message. Whatever the prehistory of individuals within the group may have been prior to that time, 2:3–4 makes clear that the audience's corporate beginnings can be traced back to their hearing the preaching of those who had first heard Christ himself preach and then had relayed Christ's message to this audience. In 3:14, the author also urges the audience to hold firm to the end the confidence that they had at the beginning, which concerned their having becoming partakers in Christ. Moreover, it is for the sake of their persevering in this same confidence (10:35–36) – a confidence clearly related to confessing Christ as high priest (10:19, 23) – that the author recalls the audience's original enlightenment and subsequent experiences in Hebrews 10:32–34. All of this evidence therefore underscores the fact that 'enlightenment' refers to the beginning point of the audience's life together as Christians, in which they must now continue to persevere in order to be saved.[14]

So, then, two particular details about this enlightenment should be noted. First, within Hebrews' world of thought, 'enlightenment' is clearly a *transitional* term describing a decisive change of situation for the audience that has a 'before' and an 'after' to it, in relation to which both author and audience can narrate other events. As 10:32 itself says, it is 'after' their 'once having been enlightened' that the audience's earliest experiences can be recounted, including various kinds of hardship that ensued as a result of it.[15] Second, the transition that this enlightenment brings about is a transition into the new covenant itself. This took place at a specific point in time, which the author can now refer to as a key juncture in their lives. In this way, it should be clear that *the first item in the list of 6:4–5 constitutes a transition- or gateway-term, describing entry into the new covenant itself.*

Of course, understanding 'enlightenment' in this way also affects how the other items in the list of 6:4–5 should be understood. In fact, Ceslas Spicq claims, with some plausibility, that all the other items in this list

[14] See also Schenck 2019: 40.

[15] For description of how this enlightenment involves a definite and momentous change, see Spicq 1952: 1: 150; Attridge 1989: 179; Lane 1991: 141; Koester 2001: 313; Schreiner 2020: 183.

actually describe the same experience as 'enlightenment'.[16] But whether or not that is true, the other items at least describe experiences that accompany or flow from this enlightenment, thereby suggesting that the other terms in the list also have new-covenant-specific associations. Evidence in the rest of the letter helps to confirm this notion.

The second item in the list is 'having tasted the heavenly gift' (*geusamenous tēs dōreas tēs epouraniou*). In the abstract, a phrase like that could describe any number of events experienced by God's people in different ages, from eating manna in the wilderness[17] to eating the Lord's Supper[18] and many others in between. However, the thematic connections within the thought-world of Hebrews itself greatly narrow the likely meaning. Of particular concern here is how the rhetoric of Hebrews strongly connects the old covenant and its ministry to the earth, and the new covenant by contrast to heaven. This characterization of the two covenants begins to emerge in a compressed form in 3:1, where the calling that the letter's new-covenant audience has received is called a 'heavenly' one (3:1) and is connected to the specific role that Jesus now plays as 'apostle and high priest of our confession'[19] in contrast to the old-covenant ministry of Moses (3:2–6). Later, though, this briefly stated contrast is developed in more detail. Especially noteworthy is the strong emphasis that the author places on how Jesus ascended as forerunner to a heavenly location (6:20) and now ministers there at God's right hand in a tabernacle that is better than the old-covenant tent specifically because it (unlike the Mosaic tent) is heavenly (8:1–2, 5; 9:11–12, 23–24). In fact, Jesus' role as high priest is so uniquely and necessarily connected to this heavenly location that 8:4 actually asserts that if Jesus ministered on earth 'he would not be a priest at all, since there are priests who offer gifts according to the law'. Clearly, this letter envisages two quite different orders of priestly ministry, one connected to earth and identified with the old covenant, and the other

---

[16] Spicq 1952: 1: 150. See also Attridge 1989: 167; Lane 1991: 141; Schenck 2019: 40.

[17] Weeks 1976: 78.

[18] Bruce (1990: 146) and Healy (2016: 118) believe that the Eucharist is at least included in this phrase. Michel (1975: 242) also believes this may be true.

[19] This is, of course, the same Jesus whom Heb. 1 – 2 already describes as being at God's right hand (1:3, 13) and having descended below the angels for a time before ascending above them (2:9). Along with 3:1, such early references make it clear that, while the more developed heaven–earth typology of the letter does not emerge until later in Hebrews (Ellingworth 1993: 320), the distinctive heavenly association of the priesthood of Christ, which is central to the new covenant itself, is nevertheless visible in the letter prior to 6:4.

inherently connected to heaven and identified with the new. In keeping with this, throughout Hebrews the efficacy of the new-covenant priesthood is also directly linked to the heavenly location of the ascended Son, to whom believers now look during their earthly sojourn (e.g. 12:1–2). By contrast, the inferiority of the old covenant is linked to its being only earthly (e.g. 12:25). So, then, while in the abstract a reference to a momentous, heavenly gift could have many different meanings, within the particular thought-world of Hebrews a strong network of associations suggests that the heavenly gift in 6:4 is new-covenant-specific. This conclusion also fits well in the particular context of 6:4, where the heavenly gift is tasted in connection with or as a result of the new-covenant experience of once having been enlightened.

Third, the author refers in 6:4 to those who have become partakers of the Holy Spirit (*metochous genēthentas pneumatos hagiou*). Interestingly, Hebrews as a whole does not speak about the Spirit as often as it speaks about heaven, but what it does say also creates important associations with the new covenant.

To be sure, a few references to the Holy Spirit in Hebrews are of a somewhat timeless nature, describing how the Spirit is the one who speaks in Scripture (3:7; 10:15) or the one who shows something (present tense) through the old-covenant ceremonies described in Scripture (9:8). In such cases, the speech or signification being described has its roots in the old-covenant period. Yet the point of specifying the Holy Spirit as the speaker or revealer of the things being described is also to accent how the words or ceremonies in view continue to be addressed (or perhaps are *especially* addressed) to Hebrews' own new-covenant audience. This is part of why present-tense verbs are used in each of these instances, to describe how the Spirit *continues* to say, show or testify to something through what was said or done before. At one level, then, these references to the Spirit's time-transcending speech through old-covenant Scripture or ceremonies show an important element of *commonality* between old and new covenants regarding the divine speech that features prominently in both (cf. 1:1–2). Yet, on another level, the rhetorical impact of these present-tense references is especially to highlight the direct and particular bearing of the Spirit's speech upon the new-covenant situation itself, as the Holy Spirit addresses Scripture 'to us' (10:15) and urges Hebrews' own audience not to lose confidence (3:6) but to enter the creation rest that is still available to them even though it was not available to some during the old-covenant period (4:1f.).

But alongside this particular set of references to the Spirit as revealer, which have some distinctive features, the balance of Hebrews' discourse about the Spirit is even more clearly and distinctively connected to the new covenant. In particular, the letter's first mention of the Spirit describes the distribution of spiritual gifts upon the audience after their first hearing of the new-covenant message from eyewitnesses of Jesus' own preaching (2:4). The fact that 2:3–4 describes the audience both hearing God's word and experiencing miracles also creates a strong connection to the content of 6:4–5, where the Spirit, the word and miracles are likewise all mentioned.[20] Later in the letter, Christ is also described as offering himself to God through the 'eternal Spirit' (9:14). This phrase should likely be taken as a reference to the Holy Spirit, as others have noted, not least because the author goes on later to describe spurning the Son's blood as an outraging of the Spirit of grace (10:29).[21] In all of these contexts, the work of the Spirit is heavily associated with the new covenant in Hebrews, and this seems particularly true of the reference in 6:4, which follows in the wake of once being enlightened and tasting a heavenly gift. In addition, there seems to be an important conceptual connection between becoming partakers of the Holy Spirit in 6:4 and being partakers of Christ in 3:14, which also describes a new-covenant-specific reality that is related to the audience's needing to hold firmly to their original confidence in Christ.

Finally in the list of Hebrews 6:4–5, the author speaks about tasting the good word of God and the powers of the age to come (*kalon geusamenous theou rhēma dynameis te mellontos aiōnos*). In general, Hebrews clearly views the word of God as something that is constantly present across all periods of history (see 1:1–2; 4:2; and elsewhere), which again underscores important features of *commonality* between old and new covenants that must never be lost sight of or downplayed, as they are crucial to the author's argument as a whole (as will be reflected upon further in subsequent chapters). Still, despite how common the word of God is to both old and new eras, the description found in 6:5 suggests that something distinctive to the new covenant is being highlighted. This is especially

[20] For some similar observations about 2:3–4 and 6:4–5, see D. E. Johnson 2018: 86.

[21] For further exegetical support see Attridge 1989: 295; Ellingworth 1993: 457, 541; Koester 2001: 415, 457; Mitchell 2007: 184, 217–218; Witherington 2007: 270–271.

evident in the way that God's word is closely connected to the powers of the age to come, since 'the goodness of the word' and 'the powers of the age to come' are both acting as objects of the same participle ('having tasted'). Moreover, this same combination of themes harks back to 2:3–4, where reception of the word was accompanied by signs, wonders and miracles (*sēmeiois te kai terasin kai poikilais dynamesin*). As mentioned before, the word that is received by the audience in 2:3–4 was clearly the climactic word first spoken by Christ (2:3; cf. 1:2) and then attested to the audience of Hebrews by those who had heard Christ (2:3). Moreover, in the larger context of that passage, this word spoken by Christ and his witnesses is directly contrasted with the old-covenant word spoken by prophets (1:1) and angels (2:2).

Along similar lines, the combination of 'word' and 'enlightenment' that is found in 6:4–5 is also worth noting, because those same themes appear again in the description of the audience's early experience in 10:32. In that context, the audience's enlightenment came about in association with their having received the knowledge of the truth (10:26), and the content of that truth again has specifically new-covenant content that is contrasted with past revelation through Moses (10:28) and led the audience to make a confession of hope in Christ, to which they must now hold fast (10:23). In all, then, while it is no doubt the case that miracles have been experienced in many time periods in redemptive history, including that of the wilderness generation of Israel,[22] nevertheless, within the thought of Hebrews, the combination of enlightenment, word of God and miracles in 6:4–5 has strong, new-covenant-specific associations and significance.

On balance, then, even with all the similarities and comparisons that may rightly be highlighted between the experiences of God's people under the old and new covenants, the associations that Hebrews itself creates with each of the items in 6:4–5 strongly suggest that this list focuses on a coherent set of experiences that are specific to the new covenant – experiences that are connected to this audience's having once been enlightened. In addition, since Hebrews 2:3–4 and 10:32–35 show that the audience of Hebrews has itself been enlightened, it seems clear that the members of that audience would have experienced the things which 6:4–5 describe.

All of this serves to underscore how poignant the warning in 6:4–6 would be for Hebrews' audience. It is of course true that 6:4–6 are written

[22] See e.g. Grudem 2000: 160; Emmrich 2003: 86.

in the third person, not the first plural or second, which helps to underscore how the passage is not directly describing Hebrews' audience as such – something that is quite important to note, since 6:6 goes on to describe the 'falling away' which the audience of Hebrews has not yet done (6:9). Still, the content of 6:4–5 clearly connects to the things that Hebrews' audience has in fact already enjoyed, specifically within the context of their hearing about and embracing the arrival of the new covenant. This not only heightens the rhetorical significance of these verses for the letter's audience; it also provides a clear conceptual context within which to turn back to the previous list in 6:1b–2 and seek to understand its particular shape and content more clearly.

6

Trying to return: going back to the old covenant alone

Having looked carefully in the previous chapter at the list found in Hebrews 6:4–5, showing that it begins with a gateway term describing transition into something new and that its content is all distinctively associated with experience of the new covenant, we now turn back to 6:1b–2 to look at a similarly constructed list there. As noted before, that list begins with repentance from dead works and also includes faith in God, instruction about washings, laying on of hands, resurrection from the dead, and eternal judgment. While some of the items mentioned in 6:1b–2, taken individually, certainly describe aspects of belief or practice that can be relevant and important to both old and new covenants, careful study will nevertheless show several things about that list that help to pinpoint its design and significance more closely. In particular, all the items in the first list are *primarily* associated with the old covenant within the thought-world of Hebrews, and some exclusively so in direct contrast to the new covenant. Conversely, none of the items identifies something distinctive of the new covenant itself in contrast to the old. As a result, the profile of the first list in 6:1b–2 stands in strong contrast to the one in 6:4–5. In addition, evidence in Hebrews strongly suggests that the items in the first list are not brought into view for the significance each might have individually but instead for how they all hold together and function as a composite unit – a coherent, alternative foundation. This has significance for understanding not only the nature of the list's content but also its larger import within the author's unfolding argument.

A list of old-covenant beliefs and practices

When looking closely at the list in Hebrews 6:1b–2, it is important to note how all of the items in this list have primary associations with the old covenant within Hebrews itself. Of course, each individual item does have its own distinct profile within the letter, and some certainly do have continuing importance in the new covenant as well, as will be shown below. On reflection, this is not surprising, since the new covenant is built with many ingredients from the old covenant and is its fulfilment. However, some of the ingredients in this list pertain to the old covenant alone, in contrast to the new. We will therefore observe a spectrum of evidence within Hebrews, and yet we will also observe an important, characteristically old-covenant character for the list as a whole, which also illuminates its interpretative significance within the thought-world of Hebrews.

When looking at one end of the spectrum of evidence, then, it is certainly the case that some items in the list are relevant to both covenants within Hebrews. Of particular note here are resurrection from the dead, eternal judgment, and faith in God. Perhaps surprisingly, though, further observation shows that even these items still have primary association with the old covenant in Hebrews, especially in the way they are specifically worded in 6:1b–2.

Looking first at 'resurrection from the dead' (*anastaseōs nekrōn*) as an example, it is important to keep in mind by way of general background information that resurrection was a stock element of belief for many Jews in the first century, including Pharisees and Essenes.[1] Belief in resurrection of the dead was certainly not peculiarly Christian in itself. Rather, what was distinctive of Christian thought was especially the claim that Jesus had already been raised, along with some distinctive theological conclusions that developed around that claim, such as those regarding his universal lordship or his being the firstfruits from the dead. However, it is also noticeable that such distinctively Christian teachings about resurrection do not feature prominently, if at all, within Hebrews' own discourse about resurrection. Instead, the topic of resurrection is spoken of in fairly traditional ways that remain relatively untransformed by specifically Christian developments.

[1] Attridge 1989: 165; Bruce 1990: 143.

When surveying the evidence in Hebrews in this respect, it stands out how Hebrews does not actually use language about resurrection very frequently, and when it does, the reference tends to be strongly linked to old-covenant belief and experience. In fact, all three express uses of a term for resurrection outside Hebrews 6:2 occur in Hebrews 11, describing the experience and expectation of believers in the old-covenant era. In 11:19, Abraham believed that God was able to raise Isaac from the dead. In 11:35, some women in the old era received their dead raised back to life, while others accepted death when persecuted because of the hope of a better resurrection in the future. Interestingly, two of these three instances refer not to final, eschatological resurrection at all but just to miraculous resuscitation back to life in this present age instead. In fact, it is only 11:35b that refers to the still-future, eschatological resurrection, and importantly even this reference comes into view specifically as an element of the future hope of people living in the old-covenant era. It is noteworthy, then, how much discourse about resurrection remains rooted in description of belief and experience within the old-covenant era in Hebrews.

Of course, it is also true that belief in Christ's own bodily resurrection comes into view by implication in Hebrews, as a necessary entailment of the author's descriptions of Christ's now being made superior to angels, who are not flesh and blood (2:5–18; 1:14), and of Christ's ascending with his own blood to appear before God (9:12, 18–24).[2] In addition, the future resurrection of new-covenant believers is implied by the way in which old-covenant believers, as they look ahead to the 'better resurrection' (11:35b), are awaiting the same perfection that new-covenant believers will also attain (11:40). So, then, the future, final resurrection of the dead is certainly a constitutive component of new-covenant hope in Hebrews.

Yet we must nevertheless keep in mind, as we grapple with the texture of Hebrews' own discourse, that the topic of resurrection does not feature nearly as prominently in that discourse, or become programmatically central to the author's topical emphases regarding what is new in the new-covenant period, as it does for example in Paul's writings.[3] Along with that, Hebrews displays no theological impulse to transform the old-covenant topic of resurrection in some of the distinctively Christian ways

[2] On the nature and importance of these themes in Hebrews, see the influential discussion throughout Moffitt 2011, esp. p. 299. See also Moffitt 2012; 2016.

[3] On the place of resurrection as a central and paradigmatically important event in Paul's thought, see esp. Gaffin 1987.

that can be observed in Pauline topoi such as viewing Christ as firstfruits (1 Cor. 15:20, 23) or as the beginning and firstborn of the general resurrection (Col. 1:18). Instead, the author's speech about resurrection fits more generically within general Jewish discourse about the topic, and this is also true of the specific wording about resurrection in Hebrews 6:2, which refers merely to belief in a resurrection at the last day.[4] In itself, then, the presence of this theme in 6:2 certainly does not show that the list in 6:1b–2 describes something particular to new-covenant belief. To the contrary, discourse about resurrection in Hebrews is rooted in and most closely associated with the old covenant, and this must be kept in mind when grappling with how this list as a whole is comprised.

Second, with regard to 'eternal judgment' (*krimatos aiōniou*), a similar set of observations pertains. As with the topic of resurrection, the author's discourse about judgment remains quite traditional, emphasizing God himself as the one who judges (10:30–31; 12:23; 13:4), rather than transforming the doctrine of final judgment to emphasize Christ himself as the one who is now appointed judge, as can sometimes be seen elsewhere in New Testament literature (e.g. Matt. 19:28; John 5:27; Rom. 2:16; 2 Cor. 5:10; 2 Tim. 4:1; Rev. 19:11–16). Throughout Hebrews, judgment is also strongly associated with the revelational content of the old covenant in particular ways, including that covenant being known for its system of retribution (2:2) and being symbolically represented by the fearsome Sinai theophany (12:18–21). To be sure, retribution, accountability and judgment also continue as topics of concern in the new-covenant period (2:3; 4:12–13; 10:30–31; 12:28–29). However, the main impact that the new covenant's arrival has on the topic of judgment in Hebrews is not regarding judgment itself but regarding avoidance of judgment, that an effective solution to God's otherwise inevitable judgment has now been provided through the efficacious priestly mediation of Christ (4:14–16; 10:19–22; 12:22–24). Alongside that, the author does anticipate a greater degree of accountability to God for members of the new covenant who fall away, due to the fuller revelation and greater experience of grace they have received in and through it, compared to the old (e.g. 2:3; 10:26–29). Still, even though the author describes Christ's appointment as worldwide ruler and king (e.g. 1:8–9; 2:5–9), this does not bring with it any emphasis on Christ himself playing the role of judge in the great assize. Instead,

[4] So too Isaacs 1992: 28 n. 2.

Christ's role when he appears a second time is especially one of saving people from God's judgment (9:28).

In general, then, the overall profile of the theme of judgment in Hebrews can be observed quite well in 12:18–25. There, judgment is associated in a particular way with the old covenant and its distinctive Sinai theophany as contrasted with the fuller expression of grace found in the new covenant. Also, God himself remains the judge of those in the new-covenant period, and yet Christ now provides the greater mediation needed in the face of judgment, which then elicits a warning to any who would not take refuge in Christ by faith. As with resurrection, therefore, the topic of eternal judgment, while present and important within both covenants, is rooted in the old covenant and remains paradigmatically associated more strongly with the old than the new.

Third, similar things must be said regarding 'faith in God' (*pisteōs epi theon*), yet with an even stronger emphasis on its connection to the old given the exact wording that the author uses to describe faith in 6:1b. Obviously, faith itself is something common to both the old- and new-covenant eras in Hebrews and something that the author urges his audience to continue having (e.g. 3:12; 4:2). This provides another example of how the relation between the old and new covenants is complex in Hebrews and includes a lot of overlap or commonality in content, which must never be overlooked or eclipsed lest their close relationship be misconstrued. Still, this does not mean that aspects of faith in the two eras cannot also be distinguished in some ways. In this regard, the specifically theocentric, rather than Christocentric, wording of the phrase 'faith in God' in 6:1 warrants some reflection. F. F. Bruce has suggested that this phraseology points particularly to the nature of faith under the old era, since for Christians 'faith in God included – or at least became tantamount to – faith in Christ'.[5] In this respect, it is worth noting how the author to the Hebrews, with his particular interest in historical progression between the covenants, characteristically describes faith in each period in ways that respect the epochal differences between them, with faith in the former era usually described in more general theological terms, compared to the more specifically Christological descriptions of those in the new.

To gain perspective on this, we can observe a contrast between Hebrews and some other New Testament authors, who more often use

[5] Bruce 1990: 141.

language that blurs the historical differences between the revelational content found in different time periods. In John 5:46, for example, Jesus says quite simply that Moses wrote about him. In 1 Corinthians 10:4, Paul says that the rock from which the Israelites drank water in the wilderness *was* Christ. Likewise, Jude 5 describes how Jesus saved a people out of Egypt. While all of these statements have great theological import, they certainly also gloss over some otherwise valid historical distinctions between earlier and later eras of biblical revelation, particularly regarding the presence and activity of Jesus Christ prior to his incarnation.

In contrast to these other authors, the author of Hebrews tends to speak with more precision about relevant differences regarding the content of faith during earlier and latter periods of God's working. In Hebrews 11, for example, he describes faith repeatedly in ways that attribute theological, more than Christological, content to the faith of those in older eras. Faith, he says, is that through which Abel offered a sacrifice to God (v. 4), Enoch pleased God (v. 5), others pleased God by believing that he exists and that he rewards those who seek him (v. 6), Abraham obeyed God's call (v. 8), Abraham looked for a heavenly city prepared by God (vv. 10, 14–16), Abraham considered that God could raise Isaac from the dead (v. 19), and Moses 'saw him who is invisible' (an apparent reference to God himself [v. 27]). Of course, at one point the author also says that by faith Moses considered 'the reproach of the Christ' to be greater wealth than the treasures of Egypt (v. 26), which may be a partial exception to the larger pattern. But even that wording is not necessarily anachronistic. It can simply indicate that Moses did not despise the reproach that was to be associated with the still-future Messiah – a thought that does not collapse the historical distance between Moses and Christ or between the old era and the new as such. It is generally true, then, that faith in the old-covenant period is described in more broadly theological, rather than Christological, terms in Hebrews.

Conversely, the author of Hebrews often gives the faith of the new-covenant period a distinctively Christ-centred content, as he again and again directs his audience's gaze towards Jesus himself. Not only does the letter focus the audience's attention on the Son[6] almost uninterruptedly

[6] Even the specific language used in 1:2–3 regarding the 'Son' helps to allow for some terminological and conceptual nuance regarding different eras. Rather than simply attributing activities such as creating and upholding the world to 'Jesus', as Jude 5 does regarding the exodus, Hebrews'

from 1:2 through to 3:6 and then repeatedly thereafter in sections about Jesus' high-priestly ministry; it also includes specific exhortations to consider Jesus (3:1), to fix one's hope on heaven where Jesus has now gone (6:19–20), to have confidence because Jesus is now the ascended high priest over God's house in heaven (10:19–21), and to run the race looking to and considering Jesus as the one who is now the founder and perfecter of the audience's faith (12:1–3). In fact, it is especially the contrast between the situations before and after the inauguration of Jesus' priestly ministry that the author points to in order to strengthen the faith of those in the new-covenant era in comparison to the lesser mediation afforded to God's people in the old era. The author emphasizes the momentous truth that, whereas believers before did not have Jesus as an active, mediating priest or as a forerunner who functions as author and perfecter of faith, now, in the new-covenant period, they do. In these ways and others, then, the historical progression between the old and new eras is quite central to this letter's description of the particular, Christological content of new-covenant belief and trust in a way that stands out from or goes beyond what pertained in the old era alone.

Given the way the author describes faith in the old and new eras, then, even though faith itself is clearly common to both old and new eras, the very generic, non-Christological mention of 'faith in God' in Hebrews 6:1 certainly fits much better with this letter's descriptions of faith during the old-covenant era than that of the new. Put differently, this description certainly does *not* highlight any of the distinctive, Christological content of new-covenant faith that is emphasized elsewhere, but instead remains entirely at home in the content of the old era.

The point, of course, is not to drive a wedge between old- and new-covenant belief, which clearly do share much in common. It is instead to seek to notice what is and is not highlighted in the list in 6:1b–2 in order to understand the nature and significance of what's found there.

Thus far, even in the case of items that are shared to some extent by old and new covenants in Hebrews' descriptions, the items in this list are still primarily associated with the old, and the wording with which they are described lacks distinctively new-covenant emphases. Of course, this

use of the term 'Son' in 1:2–3 allows for distinctions to be maintained regarding activity which the pre-incarnate Son performed before he partook of human flesh (2:14) and became qualified to serve as a human priest (2:17), and activity carried out by the incarnate Jesus subsequently.

fact also creates a strong contrast between the first list in 6:1b–2 and the second one shortly thereafter in 6:4–5, surveyed above.

Yet, while some of the items in 6:1b–2 do name topics of importance to both old and new covenants, this cannot be said for the remaining three items in the list. In fact, two of them call attention to practices strongly associated in Hebrews with aspects of the old covenant that stand in direct contrast with the new.

The clearest evidence in this regard relates to 'instruction about washings' (*baptismōn didachēs*) in 6:2.[7] Though some have interpreted this phrase as a reference to Christian baptism, many have noted how the wording in 6:2 makes that interpretation quite improbable in at least two ways. One is the specific noun used there, *baptismos*, which is certainly not typical and may in fact never be used elsewhere in the New Testament to refer to Christian baptism.[8] Another is the fact that the term 'washings' (*baptismōn*) occurs here in the plural, referring to various lustrations, whereas Christian baptism is always spoken of elsewhere in the singular.[9] As a result, it seems clear that the term 'washings' used here is not a reference to Christian baptism as such. Yet despite the strong evidence for that conclusion, some scholars have still insisted on seeing a reference to

---

[7] A few manuscripts read *didachēn* (P^{46} B 0150 d) in place of the more widely attested *didachēs*, which NA-27 and -28 side with strongly and to which UBS-5 gives an A rating. In recent scholarship, opinion has been somewhat divided between the former reading (Hughes 1977: 196 n. 34; Attridge 1989: 163; Bruce 1990: 137 n. 3, 139; Lane 1991: 132) and the latter (Solari 1970: 66; Weiss 1991: 336; Ellingworth 1993: 313–314; Koester 2001: 310 n. 177; L. T. Johnson 2006: 153; Metzger 2006: 596; Witherington 2007: 209), with some claiming that the accusative was switched to genitive to conform to surrounding genitives (e.g. Hughes, Attridge, Bruce) and others claiming that the accusative might have been preferred to provide more stylistic variety (Metzger, Witherington; cf. Ellingworth's logic). In the end, the external evidence for *didachēs* is quite strong, while arguments in either direction from internal evidence are not very strong and can cut both ways, which therefore makes *didachēs* more likely. However, even if *didachēn* were original, it is not clear that this would significantly affect the interpretation to be offered below. After all, those supporting the accusative reading typically claim that *didachēn* then becomes appositional to *themelion* in 6:1, and so, on either reading, the entire list in 6:1b–2 still functions as the direct object of *kataballomenoi* ('laying down').

[8] While there is strong textual evidence both for and against reading the noun *baptismos* rather than *baptisma* in Col. 2:12, the evidence for the former reading seems stronger. Nevertheless, this reading, if original, would still be an outlier within biblical usage and also occurs in the singular, rather than the plural. As such, Col. 2:12 does not provide strong support for what *baptismos* refers to in Heb. 6:2 (as Bruce [1990: 141] also notes).

[9] Spicq (1952: 1: 148) notes how using a plural to refer to baptism would be 'absolument insolite'. In fact, Hughes (1977: 199) points out how the reference to washings constitutes the only plural in a list otherwise comprised of singulars, which therefore makes the fact that it is plural stand out as very important to its meaning.

Christian baptism here,[10] while others have proposed that 'instruction about washings' refers to instruction about how Christian baptism differs from John the Baptist's baptism, proselyte baptism and the ceremonial washings of other Jewish sects.[11] As interesting as this latter interpretation is, however, the context in Hebrews does little to support seeing such a large conglomeration of thought in this phrase. After all, with the likely exception of Christian baptism in 10:22 (see further below), Hebrews makes no clear reference to any of the other washings just mentioned and also provides no particular analytical distinctions for defining and distinguishing John's baptism, proselyte baptism or the particular lustrations of individual Jewish sectarian groups from one another. As a result, this 'omnibus' interpretation of the phrase in 6:2 remains quite speculative and requires importing numerous category distinctions into the text that are not attested as such elsewhere in Hebrews. This lack of evidence therefore leaves the omnibus interpretation quite weak.

By contrast, Hebrews itself provides strong, positive evidence regarding what the washings in 6:2 should most plausibly be understood to mean. After all, Hebrews does actually make direct reference to washings again later, in 9:10, using the same term and again in the plural, which therefore provides the strongest contextual evidence for what the term should be taken to mean in 6:2 as well. Moreover, in 9:10 the term is clearly used to make reference to the washings practised in the Levitical sacrificial ceremonies that are distinctive in the old-covenant era in contrast to the new. In fact, the author even places specific emphasis in that context on the *plurality* of these old-covenant washings as something characteristic of the cult in that period, unlike the new, by pointing out how 'various' (*diaphorois*) they were. Given the apparent interest in the Day of Atonement in that section of the letter, the reference in 9:10 may specifically be to the numerous ceremonial washings prescribed in Leviticus for that particular day (e.g. Lev. 16:4, 20, 24, 26, 28).[12]

Whatever the case, though, it is quite clear that the plurality of the rituals contained in the Levitical system holds particular theological significance within the thought-world of Hebrews, because it helps to

[10] deSilva 2000: 218; Moffitt 2011: 184.

[11] See Solari 1970: 67; Hughes 1977: 201–202; Weiss 1991: 339; Ellingworth 1993: 315; Koester 2001: 305; L. T. Johnson 2006: 159; Witherington 2007: 210; Healy 2016: 117; Schreiner 2020: 176.

[12] Bruce (1990: 141) mentions the red heifer ceremony alluded to in Heb. 9.13, which also required various washings to be performed (Num. 19:7, 8, 9, 10).

illustrate something characteristic of the ministry in the old covenant that shows its relative ineffectiveness in contrast to the new. The same contrast regarding plurality and singularity is also seen, for example, in 7:23–24, where the fact that Levitical priests were 'many in number' helps to show the inadequacy of their ministry and of the Levitical order of priesthood itself, since its priests were continually eliminated from office by death and had to be replaced. Similarly, in 10:1–14, the fact that the Levitical sacrifices were offered repeatedly year after year also shows their ineffectiveness, since, if they had been effective, they would have ceased to be offered (v. 2). In this way of thinking, the plurality of the washings mentioned in 9:10 clearly stands out as emblematic of the old covenant's inefficacy as well and thereby suggests that the plural washings in 6:2 are also part and parcel of the old covenant and its repeated lustrations.

By contrast, the singular, once-for-all nature of the cleansing experienced by those in the new covenant is expressly highlighted in 10:22 when the author speaks of new-covenant believers 'having [their] hearts sprinkled clean [*rherantismenoi*] from an evil conscience and [their] bodies washed [*lelousmenoi*] with pure water'. The use of perfect participles in that verse, including in a likely reference to Christian baptism in the latter half of the verse, helps to accent a single definitive past action that has ongoing results for each new-covenant believer, specifically in contrast to the ineffectiveness of the plurality of washings required repeatedly in the old order.

Clearly, then, the author of Hebrews finds quite a lot of significance in the difference between plural and singular washings, since it pinpoints a crucial distinction between the ministries of the old and new eras. Within this thought-world, the plurality of 'washings' in 6:2 therefore holds a lot of significance, showing a concern for something distinctive about the old covenant over against the new. Thus, Noel Weeks is not too far from the truth when he says that the old-covenant nature of the first list in 6:1b–2 'is practically decided by the mention of "washings."'[13] Moreover, unlike with other interpretations of the phrase, there is clear, specific grounding within the narrative world of Hebrews itself for drawing this conclusion.

In addition, the next item in 6:2 also has strong connections to the peculiar nature of the old covenant in contrast to the new in Hebrews, namely 'laying on of hands' (*epitheseōs cheirōn*). Once again, in the

[13] Weeks 1976: 76.

abstract this phrase could have many different referents, depending on the thought context within which it is used, since various forms of laying on of hands were widely utilized in the ancient world. Yet, within the symbolic thought-world of Hebrews itself, the evidence is much narrower, and the activity of human hands is often associated with distinctive characteristics of the old-covenant ministry in contrast to the new. For example, in 9:11, after describing the construction of the old-covenant tabernacle, the author locates the inferiority of the Levitical ministry in the fact that it, unlike Christ's ministry, was performed in a holy place 'made by hands' (*cheiropoiētou*). In addition, the Levitical ceremonies associated with this handmade place of worship also frequently involved the laying on of hands. During the Day of Atonement itself, priests laid hands on the scapegoat as a crucial part of the rituals performed (Lev. 16:21), but the laying on of hands occurred quite frequently within the Levitical system (e.g. Exod. 29:10, 15, 19; Lev. 1:4; 3:2, 8, 13; 4:4, 15, 24, 29, 33; Num. 8:10, 12; 27:18). As a point of contrast to the new, Hebrews 9:19 describes how Moses sprinkled everything in the old-covenant priestly system with animal blood and then juxtaposes this, in 9:24, with how Christ's priestly ministry is conducted in a holy place 'not made by hands'. Again, in 12:18, the superiority of the new covenant is found in the way its worshippers, unlike those at Sinai, do not come to 'what may be touched' (*psēlaphōmenō*). In addition, the heavenly nature of Christ's ministry entails its being executed in a heavenly location (8:1–6), which 11:10 says features a city that is designed and built by God, not by human builders. It is important to note that this contrast between earthly and heavenly locations of sacrifice is quite crucial to Hebrews' world view as a whole, within which what is more real and of greater importance exists in the invisible heavens, which are by nature untouchable, as contrasted with that which is visible and earthly.[14] As the author of Hebrews sees it, then, actions performed by human hands are strongly associated with weak and impermanent results, which are therefore characteristic of the ministry of the old covenant with its earthly, touchable holy place in contrast to the ministry of the new.

Related to this, Hebrews also strongly associates the old covenant and its inefficacy with ceremonies that are performed outwardly and so have an outward effect on the body alone, rather than an inward effect on the

[14] For further explanation see e.g. Thompson 2008: 50–51.

conscience. In 9:9–10, the Levitical cult administers gifts and sacrifices that are not able to cleanse the conscience but are only 'regulations of the flesh' imposed until a future time of reformation. Importantly, these 'regulations of the flesh' specifically include the 'various washings' just commented upon above. Later, 9:13–14 builds a contrast between the sprinkling of defiled persons with animal blood for the purification of 'the flesh' under the old administration and the blood of Christ that purifies 'the conscience' in the new. In these ways, Hebrews pointedly connects the old covenant with outward ceremonial acts, especially those performed by human hands, and directly contrasts them with the new, superior ministry of Christ in the new-covenant period.

Of course, this contrast is not absolute. Hebrews does speak about the bodies of new-covenant believers 'having been washed with pure water', as mentioned earlier (10:22). However, in that context a one-time washing is connected to a once-for-all cleansing of the conscience, which pinpoints what is distinctive about the superior effect of Christ's new-covenant ministry.

By contrast, the laying on of hands in 6:2 is paired with plural washings, which clearly links it to the ineffective, outward rituals associated with the old era. In this way, the laying on of hands in 6:2 relates closely to some of the distinctive characteristics of the old-covenant ministry that stand in contrast to the greater things that have come in the new.

As a side note, while some have sought to connect the laying on of hands in 6:2 to the Christian practice that Acts associates with receiving the Spirit, this thematic connection is not evident in Hebrews. To the contrary, while the Spirit is mentioned a little later in Hebrews 6, this occurs in a separate list in 6:4, which has distinctively new-covenant content (unlike the first list) and appears in a context where it follows the paradigmatic new-covenant experience of 'enlightenment'. In this way, the progression of thought in Hebrews 6:1b–5 actually groups the laying on of hands and the experience of the Spirit separately, again suggesting that the laying on of hands is to be grouped with other items associated with the old covenant, rather than the new.[15]

On reflection, both of the central items in the list in 6:1b–2 identify aspects of the old covenant that distinguish it from the new in important

[15] As the evidence presented in this section helps to show, the lists in 6:1b–2 and 6:4–5 do not have a 'rough equivalence' as L. T. Johnson (2006: 162) suggests but actually stand in significant contrast to each other.

ways, on which the author comments directly later. When paired with the three other items studied above, which pertain to both covenants but originate within and are more strongly associated with the old, all of this gives a significantly old-covenant cast to the list as a whole.

Against that background, the only remaining item in the first list still needing consideration is 'repentance from dead works' (*metanoias apo nekrōn ergōn*) in 6:1b. Compared to many of the other terms in the two lists, language about repentance does not appear frequently in Hebrews at all. Aside from the instances in 6:1 and 6, it only shows up in 12:17 concerning Esau. Aside from being infrequent, though, the references to repentance that do occur are also relatively negative in their cast, describing part of a foundation not to re-lay (6:1), a state that people cannot be restored to (6:6) and a state that Esau did not find place for despite seeking it with tears (12:17). This pattern of usage helps to illustrate how repentance language is not something that the author of Hebrews integrates in any clear way into his positive descriptions of the Christian life or of what his audience *should* do. Perhaps surprisingly, despite all the many exhortations that the author of Hebrews issues to his audience, the exhortation to repent is not one of them.[16] He instead urges them not to re-lay a foundation headlined by repentance. This does not mean, of course, that the author is against the concept of turning away from sin towards God, which he clearly is not. But he does not voice his admonitions towards turning away from sin in the language of repentance as such. Instead, what stands out about the author's verbiage is the sparing and relatively negative use that he makes of repentance language, especially in contrast to how some other parts of the New Testament speak.

In fact, looking at the use of repentance language elsewhere in the New Testament can help to provide some perspective, since there is considerable variation between different authors or books on this score. Clearly, the language of repentance features quite prominently in the message of Jesus (see e.g. the summary of his preaching in Mark 1:15 and parallels) and in the articulation of the Christian message found in books such as Acts and Revelation.[17] Nevertheless, while *metanoia* and cognates are used quite commonly in those New Testament texts, this is by no means

---

[16] Löhr 1994: 286.

[17] Fully half of the NT's occurrences of *metanoia* appear in Luke–Acts, while 14 out of 34 occurrences of *metanoeō* also appear in Luke–Acts and another 12 in Revelation (Silva 2014: 3: 291).

universally the case. To the contrary, such terms appear only 'rarely in the Pauline writings' (Rom. 2:4–5; 2 Cor. 7:9–10; 12:21; 2 Tim. 2:25), once in the Petrine letters (2 Pet. 3:9), and not at all in other Johannine literature, or in the writings of James and Jude.[18] There is quite a lot of variety, then, regarding the extent to which various texts appropriate this particular kind of language. Moreover, within that variety, Hebrews uses the term relatively infrequently and, just as noticeably, not in ways that integrate it positively into the author's descriptions of Christian experience or growth.

More important than the mere presence or absence of repentance language, though, is the diversity that New Testament texts show regarding what this language actually refers to in various contexts. Of particular note for interpretation of Hebrews is the fact that, even within a text such as Acts, where repentance language does appear quite often to articulate the Christian message about salvation, the term 'repentance' can still be used at times to refer to something that is specific to the old covenant alone in clear *contrast* to the new.

To understand this usage in Acts, it is important to remember that the conceptual background to and precedent for Christian discourse about repentance is clearly to be found in the prophetic tradition of the Old Testament and its paradigmatically important calls for God's people to turn from rebellion back to a right relation with Israel's God (e.g. Deut. 4:30; 30:2; Neh. 1:9; Isa. 6:10; 44:22; Jer. 4:1; 5:3; Ezek. 14:6; 19:30; Hos. 14:2).[19] In New Testament testimony, this prophetic tradition also continued in the ministry of John the Baptist, who brought the old-covenant prophetic ministry to its climax with a call to repentance in preparation for the climactic new work of God in bringing the eschatological kingdom (e.g. Mark 1:4 and parallels). Evidently, the call to repentance in Scripture begins in and is strongly associated with the preparatory ministry of old-covenant prophets from Moses through John the Baptist.

In keeping with this association, it is important to note that the message of repentance can sometimes be used in the New Testament, not as a summary of the Christian message of the gospel itself, but instead

[18] Ibid. 3: 293.

[19] For a survey of evidence, see Behm and Würthwein 1964–76: 4: 975–1008; Silva 2014: 3: 290–293; Boda 2015. This evidence includes use of both *epistrephō* and its cognates, which were commonly used to describe repentance in the LXX, as well as *metanoeō* and its cognates, which came to predominate in later Jewish-Greek writings and in the NT (Silva 2014: 3: 290).

as a summary of a distinctively old-covenant message that must be distinguished historically from the apostolic message of the new era. Such distinctively old-covenant usage can be seen, for example, in Acts 19:1–7. There Paul meets some people in Ephesus who are called 'disciples' (19:1) and have already believed a message of repentance spoken by John the Baptist (19:3). But that message, while good, is clearly viewed as particular to the old era alone in contrast to the new, since it lacked the crucial content that Paul now preaches concerning the Holy Spirit (v. 2) and Jesus' coming (v. 4), for which John the Baptist's ministry had only prepared (v. 4). As a result, the faith of these disciples, while valuable, is seen as inadequate for life in the new era of apostolic preaching. Paul therefore goes on to announce to them the fulfilment of the old-covenant hope, for which these disciples' repentance had been only preparatory, and the disciples believe Paul's message about fulfilment, are given new-covenant baptism, and receive the Holy Spirit, accompanied by the authenticating testimony of tongues and prophecy (vv. 4–6).

Clearly, then, while repentance language is often used in the New Testament as part and parcel of Christian teaching, this is not always the case. It can also be used in another, distinct way, to help summarize a pattern of instruction that is particular to the old era alone and inadequate within the new. It is therefore quite important to pay careful attention to specific contexts in the New Testament in order to ascertain what repentance means and what principal associations it has.

In the specific case of Hebrews, the evidence strongly suggests that the distinctively old-covenant meaning of repentance attested in Acts 19:1–7 fits Hebrews' language and argumentation best. Not only are all of the other items in the list in 6:1b–2 associated most strongly or even exclusively with the old covenant in contrast to the new, as shown above, but also the entire list in 6:1b–2 stands in contrast to the new-covenant-specific list in 6:4–5.

At this point a striking contrast between the lists in 6:1b–2 and 6:4–5 must also be noted regarding how both lists begin. We have already seen above how 'enlightenment', which starts the second list, is a transition- or gateway-term describing a person's initial entry into right standing within the new covenant. By comparison, it bears reflection how the term 'repentance', which starts the first list, is also a transition-term in Hebrews, describing entrance into a new spiritual status. In Hebrews 12:17, for example, repentance is something that Esau sought specifically in an effort to change his status before God back to that of being an inheritor, with all the religious and covenantal implications that such a standing had within the patriarchal narrative of Genesis. 'Repentance' is not a maintenance term for Esau, then, something that would help him retain his status at the time. It instead describes something that would effect a decisive change in status for him. Again, in 6:6, repentance is in view as something that is desirable to restore someone who has fallen away back to a right standing with God. While the author says this is impossible for those he describes, the repentance under discussion is clearly in view as a gateway back into right standing, not maintaining an existing relationship, with God. Similarly in 6:1b, repentance is the first-mentioned ingredient in a purported foundation-laying process, something which is clearly a once-for-all, identity-redefining action within ancient thought. In all of these instances in Hebrews, then, repentance is not a part of mere status *maintenance*, as it might be thought of in some other contexts. In that sense, the repentance in view in Hebrews 6 is not properly understood as a mere matter of remembering 'to repent when necessary' as a matter of maintaining one's existing status before the Lord when various sins occur along the way in the Christian life, as some have thought.[20] It is instead a status-changing action, a decisive action that effects a *transition* into a different status not currently enjoyed,[21] in very much the same way that the term 'enlightenment' also functions in Hebrews.

On reflection, then, it is evidently not just the second list in Hebrews 6:4–5 but also the first one in 6:1b–2 that begins with a transition- or gateway-term, a fact which again draws the two lists into close comparison and contrast. However, while the content of the second list, including its transitional term 'having been enlightened', is all distinctively connected to the new covenant in Hebrews, the content of the first list is all strongly and sometimes exclusively associated with the old covenant in Hebrews, and its opening term 'repentance' can even be used to summarize the distinctive message of the old covenant in contrast to the new. All of this therefore helps to confirm the specifically old-covenant nature not only of the term 'repentance' in 6:1b but of the whole first list as a unit.

All told, the exegetical observations above combine to suggest that what many authors have noted in puzzlement about the list in 6:1b–2

[20] Witherington 2007: 208.

[21] On this point see also Löhr 1994: 288–289, 294.

is not circumstantial or odd but crucially important to the list's design and its significance in the argument. Schenck, like many others, comments about that list: 'these were basic Jewish beliefs, not distinctively Christian ones.'[22] On careful assessment, this observation appears to be essential for understanding the nature of the list and how it purposefully contrasts with that of the adjacent list in 6:4–5. In turn, it must also shape how we understand the function of the first list within the author's larger argument.

Reflecting again on foundations

The case has been made above for saying that the list in Hebrews 6:1b–2 consists of materials that are especially or even exclusively associated with the old covenant in Hebrews, with none that are distinctive features of the new. To understand the larger significance of this fact, we must remember how the list in 6:1b–2 comprises the contents of a foundation, and specifically one that the author urges the audience not to re-lay. At this juncture, we must therefore reflect again on the nature of foundations and the process of their construction within the ancient world.

To begin with, the fact that the contents of the list in 6:1b–2 comprise a foundation for a metaphorical building helps to confirm that the items in the list are not brought into view for the purpose of showing how each item might function individually. They are instead brought into view as a composite whole, to show how they would all function *together* to provide the basis for and define the essence of a spiritual edifice. The primary way to consider the list in 6:1b–2, then, is not by tracing the use of each term separately within Christian usage (in which some items continue to have more of a place in new-covenant belief and practice than others) but by considering the shape or character that the list as a whole possesses.

Here it is important to recall how ancient foundations were characteristically constructed not with one large stone (much less one large slab of concrete, as in modern construction) but with a collection of various stones that functioned on the basis of how well they all fitted together to work in a unified way. In such an arrangement, if even one stone was misshapen, proved weak, or did not fit well with the others and could be dislodged, the integrity and value of the foundation as a whole would

[22] Schenck 2019: 40.

be compromised. With such details in mind, Josephus comments on the necessity of carefully choosing the stones used in a foundation (Josephus, *Ant.* 8.63; *J.W.* 5.150; cf. LXX 1 Kgs 6:1; 7:10; LXX Ps. 117:22; Isa. 28:16) and how they must be carefully held together so as not to separate (*Ant.* 8.63; *J.W.* 5.150). In the event that part of a foundation did prove to be weak, though, the effectiveness of the whole foundation would be compromised, and the only remedy would be to unearth the whole thing, remove the unreliable stones and replace them with better, more dependable ones (*Ant.* 15.391).

If the audience of Hebrews was considering re-laying a foundation for themselves, then, this in itself would be a matter of grave concern to the author of Hebrews, since it would show a lack of confidence in the spiritual house that they currently inhabited, as detailed above. But the paramount concern when considering such an action would certainly be the careful selection of the exact stones to be included in the new foundation. On the one hand, which stones in their existing foundation most compromised the audience's confidence in that foundation and therefore needed to be removed? On the other hand, what other stones, which were not a part of their current foundation, could be added to help the new foundation function better than their present one? By the nature of the foundation-laying process itself, the selection of items to include or not in a new foundation was absolutely crucial, as it would allow the audience to redefine their collective essence in a way that they hoped would provide them with more confidence going forward than the foundation they were built on at present.

However, with this aspect of the ancient foundation-laying enterprise in mind, further reflection helps to show just how problematic the content of the list in 6:1b–2 is, as the author of Hebrews would see it. In particular, from the vantage point of this author, it would surely be inconceivable to redefine the community's identity using only old-covenant materials such as those listed in 6:1b–2, some of which pertain to the old era alone in contrast to the new. In fact, such an idea would not only go strongly against the message of Hebrews; it would actually be entirely without precedent in the rest of the New Testament as well.

Some reflection on New Testament discourse about foundations can help to provide a wider perspective at this juncture to contextualize the significance of the foundation described in Hebrews 6:1b–2. Naturally, New Testament descriptions of the foundation on which believers or the church stand vary somewhat in their specific details. This variety includes the fact that some descriptions of foundations do not specify the foundation's exact contents at all. It also includes how they describe the contents when they do. Yet in every instance where the content of the Christian foundation is specified, one thing remains constant: it is always described in strongly Christological terms, either by directly identifying the foundation with Christ or by identifying it with terms overtly related to him and his salvific work. For example, specifically Christological descriptions in the New Testament include identifying believers' or the church's foundation as Christ's teaching (Matt. 7:24–26), as confession of Jesus as the Christ (Matt. 16:17–18) or as Christ himself (1 Cor. 3:10–12). They also include instances where Christ is called the chief cornerstone of the foundation (Mark 12:10–11 par.; Acts 4:11; 1 Pet. 2:6–7), with his apostles and prophets sometimes constituting the other components included within the foundation (Eph. 2:20), or where the 'twelve apostles of the Lamb' constitute the whole of the foundation (Rev. 21:14). Other, more indirectly Christological descriptions still make a connection to Christ clear in context, such as when believers are said to be founded on the hope of a gospel whose content clearly centres on Christ (Col. 1:23 in the context of vv. 13–22). In fact, so consistently do New Testament authors describe foundations in direct connection to Christ that the only partial exception (outside Heb. 6) seems to be in 1 Timothy 6:19, where the foundation for a believer's future reward is his or her deeds of sacrificial giving. Even there, though, the deeds described are still part of the godliness that accords with Christ's own words (6:3) and are done in view of Christ's universal lordship (6:14–15).

In general, then, the New Testament shows a consistent pattern of describing the foundation of believers or the church in clearly new-covenant-specific terms. As much as New Testament teaching does utilize ingredients from earlier revelation, when it comes to the topic of foundation-building the emphasis in the early Christian movement was decidedly on the new things that have now come about in and through Christ. In this respect, Paul places a fine point on the matter when he insists that no one is able[23] to build on a foundation other than the one that has already been laid, namely Christ (1 Cor. 3:11).

---

[23] Interestingly, the language of inability here bears some resemblance to the language of 'impossibility' in Heb. 6:4.

Moreover, given the way in which foundations help to define the essence of the buildings they support, this pattern in New Testament descriptions is really not surprising. What has come in Christ constitutes the sum and substance of God's saving work, which then becomes the crucial benchmark defining life for God's people in the new era, the 'last of these days' (Heb. 1:2). As Hebrews itself views things, God has now spoken in a climactic, definitive way in a Son (1:2), thereby bringing about the greater, eschatological arrangement that was promised in Jeremiah 31:31–34 (cited in Heb. 8:8–12), which is new and 'not like' the old arrangement in crucial respects (Heb. 8:9). What would actually be surprising, then, would be for the defining, essential content of a Christian foundation to be drawn from old-covenant material alone.

Against this background, the non-Christological and new-covenant-*un*specific content of the foundation contemplated in Hebrews 6:1b–2 is not only entirely anomalous within the New Testament but also quite concerning. Given the strong emphasis that Hebrews places on the supremacy and necessity of Christ's redemptive work within God's plan, the fact that the letter's audience contemplates re-laying a foundation that is devoid of new-covenant content and instead includes some elements from the old covenant alone in *contrast* to the new betrays a deep problem in their thinking, as the author of Hebrews sees it. Not only is his audience tempted to start over again from the ground up, which shows a lack of confidence in their existing profession of faith; they are more specifically tempted to start over again with materials chosen from the old covenant alone *rather than the new*.

The significance of the list in Hebrews 6:1b–2 is entirely missed, then, when scholars point out ways in which various aspects of old-covenant teaching do carry over into and get incorporated into the new, or when they mention how the missionary preaching of the apostolic church derived some of its emphases from Diaspora synagogue preaching.[24] However true such claims may be, they miss the deeper significance of re-laying a foundation with materials from the old covenant alone, namely *redefining the audience's confession of faith and their grounds for confidence without reference to Christ or to the fact that the new covenant has come*. In this way, it also becomes quite clear why the author speaks as negatively

[24] Weiss 1991: 337; Thompson 2008: 133.

as he does in 6:1, urging his audience not to re-lay a foundation of this sort at all.

By implication, this also means that Hebrews 6:1b–2 does in fact communicate a direct warning to the audience not to return to and seek to start over again under the old covenant alone. Contrary to what revisionist scholars have often insisted, then, the idea that the audience of Hebrews is tempted to return from the new covenant to the old is *not* a mere matter of inference from elements found in the expository sections of the letter. Nor is it a mere product of past scholarly assumptions, whether of an anti-Jewish, supersessionist or any other kind. It is instead something that the author directly exhorts the audience not to do, which is the exact kind of evidence that some scholars consider to be the most relevant for understanding the audience's situation. Yes, the author compares and contrasts the old and new covenants and argues for the ultimate supremacy of Christ in the argumentative sections of his letter too, as all acknowledge. But is it mere conjecture that he does this because a return to the old covenant was something the audience was actually tempted to consider? The content of the author's warning in 6:1b–2 makes patently clear that it is not conjecture. Instead, the letter of Hebrews expressly identifies the temptation faced by its audience as one of leaving the new covenant, whose blessings they have already experienced, and redefining their identity instead through content provided by the old covenant alone. In this way, it should be clear that the general consensus of past scholarship is correct (even if it is for reasons quite different from those to which scholars have often appealed in the past). *Hebrews is not just arguing positively for its audience to continue going forward but is also warning and urging them not to go back to the prior, old-covenant order instead.*

As important as this conclusion is, though, it also calls for further reflection. In what sense or for what reason were the audience members attracted back to the old covenant? And why specifically does the author argue against their returning to it? What, we could ask, is 'wrong' with the old covenant in the author's view? These important questions must be answered carefully, a task to which we turn in the chapter that follows.

7

Situational change and the impossibility of return in Hebrews

We have seen so far that the members of Hebrews' audience, in the midst of a crisis of confidence regarding their profession of faith in Christ, are tempted to tear down the religious edifice they inhabit to start all over again from the ground up. We have also seen that they are specifically tempted to start over again using foundation-laying, essence-defining materials drawn exclusively from the old covenant with none specific to, and some standing in clear contrast to, the new. Moreover, the old-covenant nature of the foundation that they are tempted to re-lay stands in noticeable juxtaposition to the specifically new-covenant benefits that are described in 6:4–5, headlined by enlightenment, which have now been experienced by the audience. For this reason, the author urges the audience not to retreat from their new-covenant profession and re-lay an old-covenant-only foundation but instead to go on to maturity in Christ by heeding this letter's covenantal teaching.

Having covered this ground, we can now turn to the implications that all of this has for understanding more about the author's warning against apostasy and particularly the long-debated topic of the impossibility of people being restored to repentance after falling away, as 6:4–6 describe. Doing this will require returning to the topic of situational change as something crucial for illuminating the logic of the author's warning. As noted earlier, the warning in 6:4–6 mentions a repentance to which some might wish to be restored, and the specific wording does not suggest that this repentance, experienced before, was false or otherwise to be criticized in itself. It instead suggests that this previous repentance would be desirable to return to in theory yet is impossible to be restored to in actual fact, at least in certain situations. The question therefore arises: what in particular has changed for the people being described that makes such a return to repentance impossible? The preceding argument opens up new avenues of thought for answering this question in ways that do not rely on category distinctions that are foreign to Hebrews but actually fit quite well within the structure of Hebrews' own world of thought as evidenced in the letter itself.

Situational change and the warning passages

The epistle of Hebrews is, of course, well known for the warning passages it contains. Some of the most prominent passages containing such warnings are Hebrews 3:7 – 4:13; 6:1–8; 10:26–31; and 12:15–17.

Reflecting on such passages, Hans-Friedrich Weiss has helpfully called attention to the author's frequent use of temporal language about a progression from 'before' to 'after' that helps to contextualize and explain the warnings.[1] Starting from Weiss's observation and expanding on it, we can note a repeated pattern in the warning passages, according to which people who are described there have experienced a sequence of events that brings about an irreversible change in their situations, making their return to a previous state something that becomes impossible for them. In addition, reflecting on this pattern, especially in Hebrews 6, will help to illuminate the present situation of the Hebrews audience in more detail and so illuminate the precise nature of the author's warning as well.

To begin defining this pattern, we can first observe the overt, temporal language that the author uses regarding a progression from 'before' to 'after' in the warning of 10:26–27. There the author expressly speaks of those who go on sinning wilfully '*after* having received the knowledge of the truth' (*meta to labein tēn epignōsin tēs alētheias*). For such people, the author insists, there no longer remains a sacrifice for sins. By implication, receiving knowledge of certain truths brings about an irreversible change of situation for these people; something previously available to them now 'no longer' is, and that change is part of the 'before' and 'after' of truth reception.

It is also important to note that, in the immediate context of Hebrews 10, the truth reception at issue has a clear thematic connection to the

[1] Weiss 1991: 668.

experience of 'enlightenment' mentioned in 10:32, which marked the beginning of the Hebrews audience's new-covenant experience, and therefore to the earlier description of enlightenment in 6:4–6 as well, as many scholars note.[2] Evidently, receiving knowledge and being enlightened about the arrival of the new covenant decisively changes people's situation with regard to what options they do or do not have for relating rightly to God through sacrifice.

Clearly, too, the sacrifices at issue, which are now no longer available to those described in 10:26–27, would be the old-covenant sacrifices that have been spoken about in some detail in the preceding chapters. As Harold Attridge states, Christ's unique sacrifice 'abrogated the old cult and thus displaced any other means for reconciliation with God'.[3]

In other words, a particular person who is sinfully rejecting Christ *after* receiving knowledge about the new covenant *no longer* has old-covenant sacrifices still available to him or her as a means through which to relate rightly to God. Moreover, in view of their changed situation, the author exhorts his audience to continue their relation to God in a particular way, that is, through Christ's own blood (10:19, 29). They should not seek to rely on the old-covenant sacrifices, which are no longer available to them in an efficacious way. Naturally, this phrase 'no longer' implies that the old-covenant sacrifices *had been* available to the audience before in a way that they are not now, since they have now received the truth or been enlightened about the new covenant's arrival in Christ.

So, then, the language in 10:26–27 makes clear that a change of situation is crucially important to the logic of the warning issued there. Something available before is available no longer. Moreover, the 'before' and 'after' of the passage turn directly on a person's receiving knowledge of the new covenant, which then makes it impossible to return to the mediation of the old-covenant system.

Second, very similar, temporal language about a change from 'before' to 'after' also features importantly in the warning passage concerning Esau in 12:16–17. In that context, the author describes how Esau sold his birthright, and then specifies that 'afterwards' (*metepeita*) a new state

[2] See Michel 1975: 350; Attridge 1989: 292; Bruce 1990: 261; Lane 1991: 141; Weiss 1991: 537; deSilva 2000: 344; Grudem 2000: 176; Koester 2001: 66–67; L. T. Johnson 2006: 261; Witherington 2007: 289; Thompson 2008: 208.

[3] Attridge 1989: 293. For similar views see Ellingworth 1993: 530; Stedman 2009: 111; D. E. Johnson 2018: 153; Peterson 2020: 146; Grindheim 2023: 511; Cara 2024: 383–384.

of affairs came about in which, despite his desire to inherit the blessing and his seeking that outcome with tears, he still found no opportunity for repentance. Without getting into some of the complexities of the passage and the author's exact retelling of Esau's story,[4] it is clear that Esau's situation had decisively changed; his action of selling his birthright has the objective effect of cutting him off from the possibility of being restored to his previous state as an inheritor of blessing. Here again the author compares and contrasts two stages in someone's life. In this case, a movement from one state (being an inheritor) to another (not being an inheritor) also produces an impossibility of any return to what preceded.[5] Though the particulars of Esau's situation are somewhat different from those of the letter's audience described in Hebrews 10, the analogy between them is nevertheless quite clear, which is why the author exhorts his audience directly on the basis of Esau's experience. They are not to be like Esau, particularly in view of the irreversible change of situation that he experienced.

Third, specific language about 'before' and 'after' does not appear as such in the author's description of the wilderness generation of Israel in Hebrews 3 and 4, but concern for an irreversible change is still clearly present in what the author says about that generation's experience and in the warning that he draws from it for his own audience. Of particular note is the author's chronological interest in different 'days' or moments of opportunity that come and go along the way in Israel's story. On the one hand, the wilderness generation of Israel had once possessed a 'promise of entering [God's] rest' (4:1), but that promise was subsequently revoked. In response to the people's rebellion and unbelief expressed in their initial refusal to enter Canaan, God swore an oath that they were no longer allowed to enter the land or the rest connected to it (3:8, 18–19). Yet, on the other hand, the author speaks of 'another day' that existed later on (4:8), which is the day that David calls 'Today' in Psalm 95 and is a time period within which subsequent generations could once again enter God's rest (4:6–7). In other words, embedded in this description of 'another day' in David's time is the clear implication that a *previous* day had existed

[4] Regarding interpretative questions that arise over the peculiarities of the author's interpretation of the Esau story in Genesis, see Ellingworth 1993: 666–668.

[5] As Peterson (2020: 298) states: 'Esau . . . put himself in a position where a second chance was no longer possible.' See also Grindheim 2023: 637.

before, in the time of the wilderness generation. Yet that previous day is now over.

So, then, throughout Hebrews 3:7 – 4:13 the author describes elements of a narrative sequence that includes three distinct time periods: an initial day that existed early on in the experience of the wilderness generation when the promise of entering God's rest stood; a second period, which ensued after God had sworn that the wilderness generation could no longer enter the rest; and 'another', new day that began later, mentioned in Psalm 95, within which the opportunity to enter God's rest was available once again. As James Thompson states: 'the "today" of the psalm is actually speaking of a new day' in which 'a new opportunity to enter' is provided after the moment of opportunity for the wilderness generation itself had ended.[6] Remarkably, this new day is one which the author of Hebrews says his audience still lived within, since they too have opportunity to enter God's rest if they persevere.

In this way, even without using the same verbiage as is found in the other warning passages, Hebrews 4 nevertheless makes it clear that the wilderness generation had a specific before-and-after experience too. This entailed a decisive change of situation from the time period when the promise to enter Canaan was first given to the period when it was no longer available but had instead been revoked.[7] In fact, though the author does not overtly describe it, the total irreversibility of this change in situation for that generation is clearly entailed in Hebrews' repeated mention (3:11, 18; 4:3, 5 each time repeating the language of Ps. 95:11) of God's taking an oath, revoking his prior promise and swearing that that generation would not enter his rest. Evidently, within the Old

[6] Thompson 2008: 95; cf. Bruce 1990: 107–108; Lane 1991: 100–101. The language of God appointing a new day fits the language of Heb. 4:7–8 better than the language used by some commentators who emphasize the continuous availability of one 'ever-now, ever-new' day (L. T. Johnson 2006: 128; cf. Ellingworth 1993: 250). While God's archetypical seventh-day creation rest (referred to in 4:4) continues for ever, moments of opportunity for human beings to enter that rest can evidently come and go over the course of time. In keeping with this, the wilderness generation experienced a day when they could enter that rest and then a subsequent closing of that day. Then, later on, God again appointed another day when people could once again enter that rest, which is in fact the same day (or period of opportunity) within which the Hebrews audience itself still lived.

[7] Contra Eric Mason, who argues that Hebrews 'never utilizes this theme of reversion to an earlier existence' (2010: 12). Though the author of Hebrews never overtly mentions things such as the wilderness generation's expressed desire to go back to Egypt, as Mason notes, he does clearly explain how their going back to a situation where the promise to enter Canaan still stood became impossible due to God's oath forbidding such.

Testament narrative, this revocation was in fact final for that generation, and the impossibility of their still entering the land is seen quite vividly in Numbers 14:39–45, when those who had at first refused to go into Canaan later attempted to reverse their course and enter the land anyway. By that time, God had already solemnly sworn that that generation would not enter the land, and so their efforts to do so ended with defeat.

Thus, even without the specific verbiage about 'before' and 'after', it is clear that the wilderness generation's situation had been decisively and irreversibly altered. Their prior situation was one which they simply could not go back to,[8] in much the same way that Esau could no longer go back to being an inheritor in Hebrews 12, and a person who has been enlightened can no longer return to old-covenant sacrifices for right relation with God in Hebrews 10.

Fourth, against the backdrop of these other passages, various aspects of the language in Hebrews 6 stand out, highlighting how the warning there also addresses a change of situation. In part, the passage signals its interest in change of situation by the lengthy list of aorist participles in 6:4–5 that includes the adverb 'once' or 'once for all' (*hapax*) at the beginning. Together, these participles and their accompanying adverb describe a momentous transition that some people experience when they have been enlightened, tasted the heavenly gift, and so forth. As David deSilva notes, so much has changed for people who experience these things that it is like a different world: 'the world could no longer be seen as objectively identical to what it was for the converts before initiation.'[9] In addition, what is described in 6:4–5 clearly brings about an irreversible change in situation for those experiencing the things described there, since it now becomes impossible for such people to go back and be restored again to repentance, as verse 6 specifies. In fact, it is noteworthy in the larger context how Hebrews 6:1 and 6 both emphasize the word 'again' (*palin*) and each time in relation to the specific matter of repentance: the audience should not seek to lay *again* a foundation featuring repentance because (*gar* [v. 4]) being restored *again* to repentance is impossible after experiencing new-covenant enlightenment and then falling away.[10] Here, too, there is clearly

[8] Thompson 2008: 94.

[9] deSilva 2000: 11. Others emphasizing the momentous, once-for-all nature of the experiences listed in 6:4–5 include Attridge 1989: 12; Bruce 1990: 146; Lane 1991: 141; Ellingworth 1993: 318; Koester 2001: 66–67; L. T. Johnson 2006: 162; Witherington 2007: 212 n. 393; Schreiner 2020: 183.

[10] The idea of doing something 'again' may also come up a third time in the verb *anastaurountas*

a 'before' and 'after', just as in the other warning passages. The situation of those described in Hebrews 6 decisively changes, so that something experienced before (in this case, repentance under the old covenant) becomes impossible to return to now.

Moreover, some additional similarities between 6:4–6 and the other warning passages should be noted. As with 10:26–27, the decisive change in 6:4–6 comes about through the experience of new-covenant enlightenment. As with 12:16–17, the specific thing that cannot be returned to concerns the opportunity for repentance. The pattern of experience in each of these four passages therefore seems to be closely connected. In each one, a decisive event brings a progression from 'before' to 'after' of such a kind that a previous situation of blessing is now no longer attainable. (See Table 7.1.)

Table 7.1 Situational change leads to the impossibility of return

	Before	*After*	*Impossibility*
Wilderness generation in Heb. 3 – 4	Possessing a promise to enter God's rest	Refusing to enter in unbelief	Entering the land and the rest it typifies
Hebrews' audience in Heb. 6	Living on the old-covenant foundation headlined by repentance	Falling away after having been enlightened and experiencing new-covenant blessings	Re-laying an old foundation (6:1b) or being restored to repentance (6:6)
Hebrews' audience in Heb. 10	Living under the old covenant without knowledge of the arrival of the new	Sinning wilfully after having received knowledge of the truth (10:26) and been enlightened (10:32)	Being right with God through old-covenant sacrifices
Esau in Heb. 12	Being Isaac's heir	Selling his birthright for a single meal	Being restored to status as heir through repentance

in 6:6, which some understand to mean 'crucify again'. See Michel 1975: 244; Ellingworth 1993: 324; Mitchell 2007: 125; Witherington 2007: 215; Schreiner 2020: 188–189. However, this interpretation is disputed, with others denying that the prefix *ana-* ever means 'again' for this verb (Weeks 1976: 79; Attridge 1989: 171; Bruce 1990: 149; Weiss 1991: 346; L. T. Johnson 2006: 153; Thomas 2008: 155).

On further reflection, comparing the warning passages in Hebrews also shows that the specificity and intensity of the passages seem to increase in various ways over the course of the letter. Early on, in 2:1–5, the exhortation that the author provides is at its simplest, insisting that if unbelief in the old-covenant message delivered by angels brought retribution, the audience of Hebrews must pay even more careful attention to the new-covenant message preached by Jesus and delivered to them by eyewitnesses. There, the surrounding argument places strong emphasis on the superiority of Christ to angels, but the accompanying exhortation is stated with simple a fortiori logic and says nothing in particular about the impossibility of going back to something previous.

Then, in 3:7 – 4:16, the author strengthens his exhortation with an extended example of some who refused to believe God's promise and so were permanently shut out of entering his rest. There, the notion of an inability to return to a prior situation, in which the promise was available, is evident in the text but more by way of implication, not express statement.

By comparison, 5:11 – 6:12 advances the author's message further in several respects. For one thing, the author describes the situation of the letter's audience at greater length, including the fact that they should have made more progress by now and be able to teach, that they are presently sluggish and in spiritual danger, and that they need to move forward to the more mature understanding of Christ's Melchizedekian priesthood that the letter itself will seek to impart to them. For another thing, the author also exhorts them directly not to try to start over again with a foundation drawn from old-covenant materials alone and explains that returning through the gateway of repentance into right standing in the old is actually impossible now, after having experienced and embraced the arrival of the new.

Later, in 10:19–39, the author adds even more detail, both in his description of the audience's earlier history and in giving a more specific exhortation, urging them to draw near to God with a clean conscience through Christ, not to forsake the new-covenant assembly, but to exhort one another daily, and he also goes on to specify that if they reject Christ now, despite all that they know, there remains no other sacrifice for sins that is still available to them. In fact, he says, seeking to return to the old-covenant sacrifices would entail spurning the Son of God, profaning the blood of the new covenant and outraging the Spirit of grace.

Finally, in 12:12–17, the author tops off his exhortations through another pointed biblical example. This one concerns Esau, who clearly tried to go back to his previous state as an inheritor through the means of repentance but found no opportunity to do so, despite his tears.

On reflection, then, each section of exhortation adds additional detail, specificity and emphasis to the overall warning content in the letter. Together, they also provide further context for confirming what Hebrews 6 itself is in fact saying.

Beyond noting connections and development between passages, though, it is also important to notice some of the unique contributions that the passage in Hebrews 6 makes to the letter's overall warning content. For one thing, Hebrews 6 provides more overt language than the other passages about how the motif of the impossibility of going back to a prior state applies in the case of Hebrews' own audience. Certainly, going back to a previous state is at issue for Esau in Hebrews 12. It is also implicitly at issue in the wilderness generation's experience in Hebrews 3 – 4 and in the notion of no longer having a sacrifice for sins in Hebrews 10. Nevertheless, Hebrews 6 is the passage that details the old-covenant foundation that Hebrews' audience is tempted to return to, exhorts them against seeking to do so and categorically states that a return of this kind is impossible. In addition, Hebrews 6 also relates the impossibility of going backward directly to the relationship between the old and new covenants themselves because of how the two lists in 6:1b–2 and 4–5 are juxtaposed to each other. After all, experience of the items in the second list is specifically what makes a return through the gateway of repentance back to the old-covenant foundation in the first list impossible to do. In these ways, while the impossibility of going back to a previous state and the impossibility of returning to the old covenant are ideas clearly present in other texts, Hebrews 6 nevertheless presents these thematic elements more overtly in relation to some of the details of this audience's own situation. As a result, Hebrews 6 remains a crucial text for explaining the specific temptation at issue in Hebrews and thereby helps to confirm exactly why it is that the author focuses so much attention throughout his sermon on the relationship between the old and new covenants. After all, returning from the new to the old alone is exactly what the members of his audience are now tempted to try to do.

The impossibility of repentance revisited

These observations about the warning passages, combined with the interpretation of Hebrews 6:1–6 outlined in earlier chapters, come together to make clear exactly what the impossibility of repentance does and does not mean in 6:4–6. We saw earlier that the term 'repentance' in Hebrews 6 is used in a particular way, not to speak about remorse for sins in general or about returning again to *Christ* for forgiveness after having fallen away, but instead as the gateway into right standing under the old covenant. Given this meaning for the term 'repentance', the logic of the warning about the impossibility of repentance also becomes apparent. Just as the wilderness generation of Israel could not go back to the prior situation where the promise of rest still stood after God had rescinded his promise, just as the one who has received knowledge of and experienced the blessings of the new covenant no longer has any other sacrifice for sins available if he or she rejects Christ, and just as Esau could not go back to regain his prior position of blessing once he had decisively despised it and sold his birthright, so too those who have once been enlightened about and experienced the new-covenant blessings listed in 6:4–5 and then have fallen away cannot go back again through the gateway of repentance into right standing under the old covenant alone, even if they had previously experienced the salvific blessings of that covenant. *What they have now experienced by entering into the new covenant and its blessings brings about a decisive change in their situation that makes a return to the arrangement of the old era and its provisions impossible.*

To use the language of Hebrews 5:12 – 6:1, the author seeks to show that, while it is possible (though dangerous) for the audience to remain immature in their Christian life by drinking only milk, it is *not* possible to instead go back repentantly to the old covenant alone and have right standing before God by re-laying a foundation that uses only old-covenant materials. This would be like the disciples in Acts 19:1–7 hearing and accepting Paul's message about Christ and the Spirit, being baptized, continuing in the Christian assembly for a time and then deciding to go back to their prior standing underneath the baptism of John alone. Such a movement would surely go against the very nature of what Paul, or the author of Hebrews, believes God has now done climactically through his Son. Hebrews wants its audience to understand, then, that returning in repentance to the old covenant alone after experiencing the benefits of the new is simply not a viable possibility.

Reflecting on the significance of these exegetical conclusions, it is also important to note how this way of understanding the impossibility of repentance in Hebrews 6 provides a much better, more exegetically satisfying interpretation of the passage than previous attempts. This can be seen in how it avoids the pitfalls that beset past interpretations of the passage and satisfies the positive criteria, noted earlier, which a better interpretation would need to meet.

First, the interpretation offered above helps to provide a clear account of the author's flow of thought in Hebrews 5:11 – 6:20 as a whole. Having noted his intention of explaining Christ's Melchizedekian priesthood in 5:10, the author acknowledges that this will be difficult for the audience to understand since they are presently dull of hearing, contenting themselves with elementary teachings and therefore lacking in discernment (5:12–14). Since this state of immaturity puts them at risk spiritually, the author urges them to go on to maturity rather than entirely abandoning the spiritual house they inhabit by re-laying the foundation with old-covenant materials alone (6:1–2). He then reinforces this exhortation with both encouragement and warning. Positively, he expresses an expectation that the audience will go on to maturity with him if God permits (6:3). Negatively, he warns that the opposite course of action, returning to the old covenant through the gateway of repentance, is no longer possible for those who have been enlightened and experienced the benefits of the new covenant, since this would be tantamount to rejecting and re-crucifying Christ (6:4–6). He then extends this warning by further reflection, using scriptural language, on what happens when those receiving covenantal blessings bear fruit or not (6:7–8), before returning again to encouragement regarding his expectation for the audience to have full assurance and to inherit the promises by actually continuing forward in their Christian hope with faith and patience (6:11–12). Finally, he expands on the certainty of this hope through an exposition of promise, oath-taking, faith and patience in the case of Abraham (6:13–20), which leads back to another mention of Christ's Melchizedekian priesthood as a transition towards the more extended treatment of that topic in chapters 7–10. All of this shows how the exhortation in 6:1–2 and the severe warning in 6:4–6 fit naturally into the larger flow of the author's flow of thought.

Second, interpreting the impossibility of repentance as described above does not require narrowing or softening the meaning of the text in ways that conflict with its own strong and unqualified wording. In that respect, it does not seek to create a loophole by saying that restoration to repentance is impossible humanly speaking but not for God, when such a qualification is not only absent in the passage but also goes against the author's general usage of language about impossibility. It also does not allege that the author's language is merely hyperbolic, with all the pastoral short-sightedness that such an exaggerated overstatement would inevitably entail. It instead takes the categorical nature of the statement in 6:4–6 at full value, exactly as worded. The meaning of the statement just needs to be understood more precisely in relation to the author's comparison and contrast of the old- and new-covenant orders as a whole.

Third, the interpretation above does not focus on category distinctions that are unstated in or even foreign to Hebrews 6 and Hebrews as a whole. It does not, for example, allege that the author is focused only on corporate disobedience and judgment rather than individual, or temporal rewards rather than eternal life, both of which interpretations import distinctions that go against the grain of the immediate and larger contexts. It also does not centre on assertions regarding divine election, true or false conversion, a uniquely hardened subjective state for some apostates, or a specially defined kind of apostasy that prohibits someone from returning to Christ – none of which are borne out by the context. To the contrary, the interpretation defended here focuses on the relationship of and distinction between the old and new covenants, which is clearly at issue in Hebrews 6 itself and is also such a programmatically important concern within the sermon's larger argument (as will be discussed further in the next chapter).

Fourth, the interpretation above clearly answers the question posed early in this study regarding situational change, explaining why the repentance mentioned in 6:6 is not critiqued (as if it were an invalid, false repentance to begin with) but is still said to be impossible to return to a second time. At issue in this passage is not the lack of genuineness of the first repentance, which would make it undesirable and soterically irrelevant to consider repeating anyway, but the historical progression from old covenant to new and a given person's knowledge about and experience of that great, epochal change. At the juncture in a person's individual experience when they are enlightened, the great, objective change that has come about in history through God's climactic last-day speech, Christ's sacrificial death, and his ascension as high priest into the heavenly tabernacle all produce a change in the life history of an individual person's existence too. Having now learned about and tasted of the new covenant, a given person's situation has changed decisively for the better, so long as they continue in their original confidence, approaching the throne of God through Christ to find help and grace. But their situation has also changed in another way, in that it has now become impossible for them to go back and stand in right relation to God through the pattern of belief and practice that God himself had previously provided in the old covenant. To be sure, this statement calls for further explanation regarding the precise relationship between the old and new covenants, which will be offered in the next chapter. But the mere fact that this change has come about, wherein new-covenant enlightenment has rendered something previously experienced now impossible to return to, is patent from the very wording of 6:4–6 itself, and the interpretation above helps to make better sense of that than previous attempts at analysing it.

Fifth, the interpretation above also shows that the impossibility of repentance does *not* mean the impossibility of returning to *Christ* to receive forgiveness again through him after falling away, and to say otherwise goes far beyond what this or any of the other warning passages in Hebrews states. The passage instead points out that someone who falls away from Christ cannot return to right standing with God through the old covenant alone in distinction from the new.

Technically speaking, the question of whether an apostate of any sort could return to *Christ* again after falling away does not seem to be something that Hebrews comments upon directly, so far as I can see, and this is largely because of the particular situation the author is addressing. Of central importance here is the clear fact that the audience of Hebrews had *not* actually apostatized when the letter was written, and the author also remained hopeful that they would not do so (6:9–12). In such a situation, it would have been very odd for the author to tell them ahead of time that, if they do in fact apostatize, they can still return to Christ later, as if to offer them a future contingency plan or comfort them that the consequences of falling away could be ameliorated after the fact. Instead, the author sensibly focuses entirely on dissuading the audience from the particular kind of apostasy they are tempted to fall into, namely returning from the new covenant to the old alone, and therefore on making a clear argument for saying that they should *remain* in Christ and continue in the same confidence they have had since their enlightenment, because what they have now in the new covenant is far better than (and in fact the intended fulfilment of) what came before anyway. Given this argumentative focus, an answer regarding whether an apostate can turn back to Christ and be forgiven is not directly provided one way or the other in Hebrews.

At the same time, however, even though Hebrews does not directly address that topic, some inferences might also be drawn about it from what Hebrews does say. Looking in one direction, it seems likely within the thought-world of Hebrews that a person who had fallen away from the *old* covenant and did not yet *know* about the coming of the new might legitimately be urged to return in repentance to the provisions of the old covenant itself and to continue waiting faithfully for the coming of the new, just as many prophets of old had always urged. The legitimacy of such an exhortation for a person who knows only of the old covenant might be surmised indirectly from the fact that repentance, as an entry into right standing in the old covenant, is *not* critiqued in Hebrews, as if it never had any benefit. Rather, as observed before, the repentance that the audience had experienced before is assumed to have had great value in its own time, but is simply said to be historically outmoded and impossible to return to for those who have now entered the new covenant. Looking in another direction, though, what Hebrews teaches also suggests that a person who has fallen away from the *new* covenant, though unable to return in repentance to the old alone, should nevertheless be urged to come back to Christ again, since Christ alone has provided the once-for-all, efficacious sacrifice that truly cleanses the conscience in the way that is needed when standing before the judgment seat of God. On reflection, this is where the 'Christ alone' interpretation of Hebrews 6, though insufficient for explaining the passage as a whole, is still quite correct in its emphasis, since it helpfully captures some of the soteriological implications of Hebrews' broader teaching. Indeed, God's last-day message and final sacrifice has now come through Christ. Where else could anyone conceivably turn, then, even after apostatizing, to be saved from the coming judgment?

Whether or not these inferences regarding a return to Christ after apostasy are correct, it should at least be clear that interpreting the impossibility of repentance in the covenantal way described above – as a statement of the categorical impossibility of a return from the new covenant to the old alone – makes most sense of the wording of Hebrews 6:4–6 within both the immediate and broader contexts. At the same time, even as this much becomes clear, further questions linger about the precise logic behind *why* the author believes a return to the old covenant is impossible and how that claim fits into the fabric of Hebrews' larger thinking.

At this juncture, it becomes important to delve more deeply into the relationship between the old and new covenants as Hebrews sees it and to seek clarity about what this author does and does not say 'against' the former. This will be addressed in the next chapter.

8
Relating the covenants: the deeper logic of Hebrews' argument

The preceding chapters have argued, among other things, that the audience of Hebrews is in fact tempted to go backward to start all over again in the old covenant alone and that the author of Hebrews is urgently warning them not to do so, saying that it is actually impossible to be in right relation with God in this way after they have been enlightened about and experienced the blessings of the new covenant. In that sense, Hebrews is arguing not only in favour of something positive (going forward into maturity in one's Christian profession) but also against something else (a return to the old covenant).

Yet this way of framing Hebrews' argument brings up various questions regarding why and in what sense the author juxtaposes or contrasts the old and new covenants. In part, this topic is of concern in relation to unduly polemical, dismissive or even anti-Jewish views of the old covenant in Hebrews scholarship, as previously discussed. For this and other reasons, it is important to reflect more deeply on the logic of the sermon's argument, in particular to appreciate the balance that the letter displays. While the author is very concerned that the audience not return to the old covenant and believes that would be disastrous, he nevertheless views that covenant quite positively overall, seeing it as a good and gracious provision of God in its time and something which stands in essential continuity with the new covenant – in fact, something of which the new is a further extension and completion in crucial respects. At the same time, a question in the other direction must be addressed: wherein does the contrast between the old and new covenants really lie in Hebrews, and why does the author both appreciate the old *and* argue against its continued use, at one and the same time? Or, put differently, how is it that the author argues against returning to the old but does not view the old disparagingly or dismissively?

Gracious covenants and an existentially loaded question

At the outset, it is important to note that Hebrews does not present the old and new covenants as having contrasting soteriologies of works and grace. Rather, the descriptions of the old covenant in general and of the old foundation that the audience is tempted to re-lay in 6:1b–2 in particular are in fact characterized by their gracious nature.

This is clear in the language of 6:1b, where the old foundation, which the audience members are tempted to start over with, is headlined by both 'repentance from dead works' and 'faith in God', which already suggests that the 'problem' with the old covenant is not found in its being legalistic or works-based. As Kenneth Schenck notes, most scholars today view the phrase 'dead works' as indicating works that lead to death because they are sinful in their nature.[1] This would be in keeping with how 9:14 later describes the blood of Christ cleansing people from 'dead works' so that they can serve the living God. Unfortunately, some have wrongly identified the 'dead works' in 9:14 with the external regulations of the Levitical cult,[2] but those regulations themselves are not something from which people must be cleansed. They are instead something that provided a legitimate but limited, outward cleansing, as will be discussed later below. It is better, then, to understand 'dead works' in both 9:14 and 6:1b as referring to sinful deeds that deserve death. Understood in this way, repentance from such works in 6:1b involves turning away from sinful deeds and the fearful judgment that they would otherwise incur and turning instead to God for forgiveness. By comparison, 'faith in God' entails trust or reliance on God for 'creation out of nothing, life

[1] Schenck 2007: 19. Those taking this view include Hughes 1977: 197; Attridge 1989: 164; Bruce 1990: 140; Koester 2001: 304; Mitchell 2007: 119; Boda 2015: 175; Healy 2016: 116; Schreiner 2020: 175. This consensus stands in contrast to an older view that 'dead works' refers specifically to idol worship (on appeal to texts such as Wisd. 15:17) and that this shows that the audience of Hebrews was Gentile (see e.g. Schenck 2003: 93; 2007: 194, 198 n. 2; more recently, see Whitlark 2014: 61–75; Martin and Whitlark 2023: 355–356). Against the logic of that view, see Bruce 1990: 5; deSilva 2000: 216–217.

[2] E.g. Solari 1970: 64; Lane 1991: 140. Similarly, Healy 2016: 116.

out of death, salvation in place of judgment'.[3] So, then, whatever the exact problem is with the old-covenant foundation that the author urges his audience not to re-lay, nothing suggests that the problem is its being legalistic. Instead, the leading components of this foundation involve recognizing and eschewing one's own sinful deeds that deserve judgment and seeking eternal life instead through trust in God himself.

Moreover, if the 'washings' and 'laying on of hands' that are also part of the old covenant foundation in 6:1b–2 refer to ritual actions described in the Levitical law, as argued above, this too points towards the grace-based nature of the old-covenant foundation. Indeed, the substance of the old-covenant Levitical system, as Hebrews describes it, particularly centres on the provision of atonement for sin through sacrifice, to which the ablutionary practices of the old covenant are ritually and symbolically connected. In this respect, the core concern of the old-covenant system of purity is summarized in 9:22, when the author says: 'under the law almost everything is purified with blood, and without the shedding of blood there is no remission of sins.' The whole old-covenant economy is thereby styled as a way that God provided for avoiding judgment by graciously appointing blood sacrifices in order to deal with the sins of the people (7:27; 9:7). Everything about the old covenant in general and the old-covenant foundation in 6:1b–2 therefore shows a concern for obtaining God's mercy to atone for sin and provide an otherwise undeserved reprieve from judgment and entrance into God's heavenly presence and blessing.

So, then, while it is true that the efficacy of the old-covenant priestly system was limited, it was nevertheless a genuine if 'limited *means* for dealing with sin', just as the new-covenant death of Christ was 'the definitive *means*', that is, the full and final means, for doing the same thing.[4] Whatever a writer such as the apostle Paul may mean by saying that the 'letter' associated with the old covenant kills while the Spirit associated with the new covenant makes alive (2 Cor. 3:6), or by pitting law against grace (Rom. 6:14), and whatever should be made of the varying constructions of grace and works among first-century Jews that provoked controversies between Paul and some of his Jewish contemporaries (e.g. Gal. 2:11–16; 6:12–14), the author of Hebrews for his part does not

[3] Alexander 2009: 406; cf. Schreiner 2020: 176.

[4] Koester 2001: 110.

present the old and new covenants in a fundamentally contrasting way soteriologically but as cordially founded in and thoroughly characterized by – indeed, systems given by God for providing – gracious atonement. Importantly, then, the contrasts that the author makes between old and new covenants are not contrasts between works and grace but between *grace and grace*.

At the same time, while Hebrews does not present the contrast between old and new covenants as one of works and grace, it also does not present it as centred in conflicts regarding ethnicity or social boundaries. As noted earlier, Hebrews never even mentions the terms 'Jew' and 'Gentile' as such and shows no direct concern for notable communal 'boundary-markers' such as circumcision, holy days or the general practice of kosher laws in the home. Such topics, which are of constitutive importance for defining a Jewish social identity over against a Gentile one, do not appear to be of significant concern to this author. In fact, when Hebrews does point out a contrast regarding the kinds of table fellowship that different sets of people enjoy, the contrast is specifically between food fellowship at God's heavenly altar and the food fellowship enjoyed by those who serve the old-covenant tent (13:10). This contrasts an earthly table-fellowship with a heavenly one. It also focuses on a contrast between Hebrews' audience and old-covenant *priests*, not between the audience and the household table-fellowship of other Jews in general. In addition, as many have noted, Hebrews certainly does not object to the Jewishness of the old covenant. Instead, those whom Christ came to help are described en masse as the seed of Abraham (2:16),[5] and positive examples of proper faith, which the audience should imitate, are regularly drawn from the old covenant (Heb. 11). Moreover, as Eric Mason points out, the negative examples drawn from the old covenant are not negative 'because [the people involved] were Hebrew or under the Sinai law' but because of their hard-heartedness at that time.[6] Indeed, as Schenck says, the key categories with which the author theologizes throughout his letter are thoroughly Jewish, and the audience, as part of the Christian assembly of worship, are viewed in essential continuity with Israel.[7]

[5] Schenck 2019: 19.

[6] Mason 2010: 12.

[7] Schenck 2019: 197.

On balance, then, while the 'problem' with the old covenant is not works-righteousness in Hebrews, neither is it ethnocentrism or a matter of how Jews and Gentiles should relate to one another socially. In this way, neither the problems typically associated with Old Perspective interpretation nor those associated with much New Perspective interpretation[8] seem to identify what is most at issue for the author of Hebrews when he navigates the relationship of the old and new covenants and speaks against a renewed reliance on the old.

Yet more must be said to clarify the picture further. Not only does Hebrews *not* contrast the old and new covenants over matters related to either works-righteousness or ethnic exclusivism, it instead presents the old and new as so closely related to each other as to be made of essentially the same cloth. This is clear, for example, from the fact that both Moses and Jesus served the same house, with Moses ministering in that house as servant, Jesus serving over the house as Son, and the audience of Hebrews comprising part of that house (3:3–6).[9] In other words, Moses and the new-covenant audience are ultimately part of the same enterprise, not different ones, and Moses helps to *serve* the new-covenant audience. In addition, old-covenant Israel and the audience of Hebrews are described as part of the same people (4:9)[10] and as living on the basis of and seeking the fulfilment of the same promise of rest (4:1, 2, 9).[11] Similarly, not only are those in the old covenant used as examples of faith for those in the new covenant to imitate (esp. Heb. 11), but the ultimate blessing that old-covenant faith looked forward to is the same as what new-covenant believers also seek and will receive, namely dwelling in the eternal, heavenly country or in the city built by God (11:10, 16; cf. 12:1, 2; 13:14).[12] In fact, all throughout Hebrews, figures or events in the old period regularly provide the positive template after which those in the new covenant are patterned, such as when Christ comes in the likeness of the ancient

[8] For surveys of views related to Old and New Perspective interpretative approaches, especially those related to Pauline studies, see Westerholm 2004: 101–258; Watson 2007: 1–56; Yinger 2011. For reflections on these debates with a view to Hebrews, see Schenck 2019: 1–23.

[9] See Attridge 1989: 111; Ellingworth 1993: 203, 210; Mitchell 2007: 89; Witherington 2007: 170.

[10] See L. T. Johnson 2006: 129; Mitchell 2007: 99. As Lane says: 'The writer's constant reflection on Scripture presupposes continuity with "old Israel"' (1991: cxxvii); cf. Ellingworth 1993: 24.

[11] See Ellingworth 1993: 238; Koester 2001: 110–112; Mitchell 2007: 96; Thompson 2008: 94.

[12] See Attridge 1989: 324; Bruce 1990: 294, 301; Ellingworth 1993: 585; L. T. Johnson 2006: 310; Mitchell 2007: 27; Witherington 2007: 25–26; Thompson 2008: 247; Schreiner 2020: 33.

Melchizedek (7:14–17; cf. 5:6, 10; 6:20; 7:11)[13] or when the ascension and priestly ministry of Christ are understood in comparison with the work of the high priests in the tabernacle on the Day of Atonement (9:1–14).[14] In these ways and others, the old and new covenants are quite closely and cordially related in Hebrews, with both resembling each other and essentially serving the same goal through similar means.

And yet, on reflection, while all of these things show how the old and new covenants are not pitted against each other in Hebrews, they also serve to put an even finer point on the question posed above: why, if the two covenants are so *similar*, does the author still think it necessary not only to recommend the new over the old but also to solemnly *warn* the audience not to return to reliance on the old alone? Why, if both covenants not only are gracious but also help to deliver the same ultimate blessing, is the spectre of a return to the old put in such grave terms as seen in 6:4–6 or 10:26–31? In point of fact, the intricate similarities between the old and new covenants that the author himself details in this sermon no doubt help to identify why its recipients feel the precise tension that they do regarding the possibility of returning. Put simply, if the good, gracious old covenant, given by God through angels, was good enough for Moses, David and many others to live under during the old era, why can it not be good enough once again for this letter's audience now?

Yet even this way of asking the question may not describe the full tension that the audience feels. Another layer to the audience's situation may also be reflected within the letter, which would heighten the tension they feel in a particularly existential way. In this regard, we can observe how some of the language found in Hebrews makes it seem quite likely that the question about the continued viability of the old covenant was far from being merely theoretical for the audience, rooted in a theological construct about how the two covenants relate, but instead had a poignantly *autobiographical* dimension to it for them as well, being rooted in their own prior experience of life underneath the old system. While the author of Hebrews is notoriously sparing with information about his

[13] See Attridge 1989: 199, 202; Lane 1991: 183–184.

[14] See Attridge 1989: 231; Ellingworth 1993: 420. Of course, the patterning or typological relationship in Hebrews is actually more complex than this, since many old-covenant realities were themselves patterned after pre-existing heavenly realities (e.g. 7:3 regarding Melchizedek himself coming in the likeness of the Son of God and 8:5 regarding the old-covenant tabernacle being patterned after the pre-existent heavenly tabernacle). For further discussion see Vos 1956: 55–65.

audience's background, we saw earlier how the warning passages of the letter do frequently speak about the impossibility of a given set of people going *back to a prior state* that they themselves had experienced previously. Esau, for example, desired to be restored to his own prior position of being one who would inherit blessing. The wilderness generation too desired to go back to the prior day when the promise to enter God's rest was still valid for them. With these people's experience in mind, it also stands out how the warnings in Hebrews 6 are specifically worded in terms of laying 'again' a foundation from the old covenant (6:1b) or being restored 'again' to repentance (6:6). As was the case with the other warning passages, this language concerns the notion of going back a second time to something possessed or experienced before. Yet in Hebrews 6, it is the audience's own situation that is more directly in view.

So, then, while this sequential language of going back again *could* be read as having a generically historical reference, describing how the audience was contemplating re-laying the foundation that had once functioned so well for God's people *in general* in the past, the wording of the other warning passages, the poignant content of the exhortation in Hebrews 6 and the overall logic of the letter's argument all make it *more likely* that something more personal to this letter's audience is in view – that the audience of Hebrews is contemplating returning to the old-covenant belief and practice that *they themselves had previously experienced*, prior to having learned about and embraced the arrival of the new. In other words, the word 'again' in these verses may show – and in fact, seems most likely to show – *that the members of this audience (like the disciples in Acts 19:1–7) had once lived in a posture of repentance and faith under the old-covenant economy and experienced its blessings for themselves.*

If so, then the existential tension wrapped up in the question of whether to lay 'again' an old-covenant-only foundation would be all the more palpable and concrete to them. The question before them would not *only* be why the form of grace that had sufficed for Moses, David and others before could not be good enough for them now, but more particularly why the form of grace that had sufficed for and sustained *the audience themselves* before was not sufficient to return to a second time now.

In the end, whether it is a return to their own past experience of the old or just a return to the experience of others in generations past that is at issue with the audience, the gracious nature of that old-covenant foundation is clearly something that the author of Hebrews affirms, as is the gracious nature of the very foundation described in 6:1b–2 which the audience is considering re-laying for themselves. All of this is no doubt part of what made the whole idea of going back to the old seem both plausible and attractive to the audience in the first place. The decision between persevering in the new or going back to the old is not a decision between grace and *works* but between grace and *grace*, that is, between two distinct but essentially similar systems for relating to God in humble reliance on his undeserved mercy and the atonement that he himself provides.

The relation of the covenants and the logic of Hebrews' warning

While noting the gracious nature of both old and new covenants in Hebrews is crucial for understanding the letter's theology, it also draws even more attention to the fact that the author considers re-laying a foundation in the gracious old covenant *impossible* for his audience to do – in fact he views it as something that would bring disastrous consequences, and he strongly exhorts them against doing it. Given the essentially gracious nature of the old covenant, we must ask ourselves precisely why this is so. The reason, all things told, lies in the deeper logic of Hebrews' argument, which not only presents the two covenants as each dispensing grace and helping to impart the same ultimate blessing, but also sees them having a very specific kind of relationship to each other. In particular, while each covenant is of the same substance, *the old was purposefully designed as preparatory to the new and so was inherently temporary and salvifically inadequate from its inception.*

Though it is certainly the case that Hebrews' comparisons between old and new covenants are generally positive and appreciative, comparing something good to something even better (not something bad to something good), it is also true that the author sees the good old covenant as having decisive limits in regard to what it could ever accomplish. Most notably with regard to the very central topic of atonement, the blood atonement prescribed under the old covenant, though still very much a gracious provision of God in its time, nevertheless provided only outward cleansing of the flesh, according to Hebrews' descriptions, rather than the inward cleansing of the conscience that is most needed by sinful people (9:9).[15] The efficacy of the sacrifices offered under the old covenant was also limited because the sacrifices were only offered in the earthly, not the heavenly, tabernacle.[16] In addition, their atoning effect was temporary, since otherwise the animal sacrifices would not have been offered repeatedly each year, unlike Christ's once-for-all offering (10:1–2, 10–14).[17] Similar limitations can also be observed regarding the intercession provided under the old covenant. On the one hand, the mediation of the old-covenant priests was only temporary, since those priests each eventually died, and it was also performed by sinful men who had to offer sacrifices for their own sins first. On the other hand, the mediation of the sinless Christ is permanent, unchanging and full of ineffable power (see 7:15–28; 13:8).[18]

In the view of the author of Hebrews, then, the old-covenant priestly system was *both* good *and* inadequate to provide the full measure of what God's people ultimately need in order to be saved from sin. According to this logic, believers under the old covenant do not actually receive ultimate blessing or full perfection other than through the work of Christ (which was still future to them [11:39–40]).[19] Moreover, all of these elements of inadequacy pertain within the old covenant quite apart from any mention (whether retrospectively or prospectively) of the temple itself being destroyed, or even, we might add, of the possibility of its ever being rebuilt subsequently. The basis for asserting the inadequacy of the atonement provided in the old covenant simply lies elsewhere, as Hebrews describes it.

Given this view of the old covenant in comparison to the new, the implications for the author's argument are significant. To return from the

[15] L. T. Johnson (2006: 226) notes how outward application of cleansing cannot be most decisive, given the Platonic aspects of the writer's thought that prioritize the inward and invisible. See also Ellingworth 1993: 439; deSilva 2000: 301; Koester 2001: 112; Mitchell 2007: 23; Schreiner 2020: 42.

[16] Thompson (2008: 185) notes how Hebrews views earthly sacrifices as 'fundamentally ineffective' for full atonement. See also Koester 2001:112; Schreiner 2020: 42.

[17] See Lane 1991: ci; Ellingworth 1993: 489, 493–494; deSilva 2000: 317; Mitchell 2007: 23; Thompson 2008: 194; Schreiner 2020: 43. Ellingworth (1993: 439) further claims that the old-covenant sacrifices had efficacy only within this present age, not in the age to come.

[18] See Bruce 1990: 169; Lane 1991: ci; deSilva 2000: 273–274; Koester 2001: 112; Thompson 2008: 157, 162.

[19] As Ellingworth says: 'Men and women of the OT were given promises which received at that time a limited fulfillment, but . . . the completion of God's purpose is found in Jesus' (1993: 239). Koester (2001: 110, 113) also notes how people in the old covenant only enter into glory or full and final relationship with God through the provisions of Christ in the new covenant. See also Attridge 1989: 352; Bruce 1990: 330; L. T. Johnson 2006: 290; Witherington 2007: 25–26.

provision of the new covenant to that of the old would be to return from something that provides the full, permanent cleansing of the conscience before a holy God, which is necessary for being perfected and avoiding ultimate judgment, to something lesser that did not and was never designed to provide that. This, as the author sees it, would be an inherently tragic and fatal turn.

Along with this, to fully appreciate the author's argument about not returning to the old covenant, it is important to appreciate not only the inferiority of the old covenant compared to the new with respect to atonement but also how the former covenant is purposefully designed as *preparatory* to the latter, something meant to point ahead towards and lead to the greater substance that the new would eventually bring. This way of thinking is especially evident in the author's conception of the old covenant as containing copies, types or shadows of the ultimate originals, antitypes or true forms that are found in the new.

On this topic, several of the author's descriptions of the old- and new-covenant ministries prove to be especially significant. For example, having described Christ as high priest in heaven and having contrasted him with the Levitical priests who serve in the tabernacle on earth, the author says that the old-covenant priests 'serve a copy and shadow of the heavenly things' (8:5). In that conception, the earthly tabernacle set up by Moses was designed from the outset to resemble God's own abode in heaven, which the author describes as the original, greater tabernacle. But, while the Levitical priests served in a holy space that was a mere earthly copy or replica of God's own dwelling in heaven, Christ's ministry involved ascending into the original tabernacle space in heaven itself with his own blood, which was shed during his crucifixion on earth (9:11–12). Similarly, not only is the earthly tabernacle as a whole considered to be a copy of the heavenly space, but the vessels and articles in the earthly tabernacle, which needed to be ritually cleansed with animal blood in the Levitical system, are also called 'copies' of the 'heavenly things' (9:23) or of the 'true things' (9:24). Again, later, the whole priestly system given through the Mosaic law is called a 'shadow of the good things to come' in the new covenant, and as a mere shadow the old covenant did not contain 'the very form of the things' (*autēn tēn eikona tōn pragmatōn* [10:1]).[20]

[20] For discussion of the conception in these passages, see esp. Attridge 1989: 219, 263, 270–271.

Importantly, when the ministries of the two covenants are understood to relate to each other along these lines, the value of the old-covenant ministry especially consists of its role in foreshadowing and *leading to* the greater things that follow after it. Conversely, the greater things in the new covenant are the ones that actually accomplish the full atonement and mediation that the old had pointed towards but could not itself provide. In other words, the new covenant brings full, qualitatively lasting – that is to say, eschatological – content, which was only pointed towards or typified in the sub-eschatological old-covenant arrangement.

Yet, while these features of Hebrews' conception of the two covenants are overtly stated in the letter and widely noted by scholars, their implications for the topic of returning to the old covenant have not been adequately explored. For example, according to Schenck, the fact that the author warns his audience in 3:12 against 'turning away from the living God' implies that the audience is not tempted to turn from Christianity to Judaism, since the living God is also worshipped in Judaism. Instead, he reasons, it must be an exhortation against turning away from the whole Judeo-Christian tradition to mere paganism.[21] Likewise, Mason argues that the problem that Hebrews addresses is a threat to maintaining faith at all, not the threat of turning from one form of faith (that of Christianity) to another (that of non-Christian Judaism).[22] In other words, these authors believe that the old covenant was so similar to the new that returning to it would not entail a radical enough breach with the audience's current profession of faith to warrant the strong warnings given by the author. To similar effect, others have argued on social grounds that it makes no sense to view the audience of Hebrews as being tempted to 'return' to Judaism because, sociologically speaking, Christianity had not yet departed from Judaism at the time when Hebrews was written. In other words, how could one return to something one had not left?[23] Whether factored in terms of soteriological content (faith and grace) or social relations (the extent to which Christianity was not yet separate from Judaism), both these lines of thought emphasize the degree of continuity between the old

---

[21] Schenck 2019: 20, 21, 38. In addition to other sorts of response made below, it is useful to note what D. A. Carson and Douglas Moo (2005: 610) observe, i.e. language about turning away from the living God is originally used in 3:12 to describe what specific Jews, namely those in the wilderness generation of Israel, had done before. This makes it clear that such a turning is not something only Gentiles are capable of; it can be done by unbelieving Jews as well.

[22] Mason 2010: 9.

[23] See Lane 1991: cxxxiv; Hooker 2009: 190–191.

and the new and use it as a reason why return to the old is not actually the problem that Hebrews is addressing.

However, as attractive as it is to see the old and new covenants as merely in harmony with each other with no possibility of conflict between them, the problem with the views just described is that they fail to adequately reckon with the difference between moving *forward* from faith under the old covenant to faith under the new, on the one hand, and seeking to move *backward* from faith in the new covenant to faith in the old *only*, on the other hand. Given the very nature of the two covenants, as Hebrews itself describes them, these two directions of movement are quite different and, in fact, diametrically opposite in their effects. After all, movement forward from old to new clearly accords with the God-given design of the covenants as Hebrews describes it. But movement backward from the new to the old goes against the design of the covenants in general and involves not just holding on to the old but reverting to it *instead of or as an alternative to the new*.

As Hebrews sees things, though, the atonement provided in the new-covenant work of Christ was necessary from the beginning – something which the old always called for and to which it was inherently designed to lead, since the old alone never provided the full, inward cleansing that is ultimately needed for salvation. Certainly, believers under the old covenant did know and serve the living God, and they were rightly related to him through repentance, faith, and the grace signified by laying on of hands, various washings and other gracious provisions within that system. Certainly, too, all of this was decidedly beneficial, something that imparted a true hope for inheritance in the ultimate heavenly city (which members of the new covenant also await). In these ways, the old-covenant system was clearly no 'threat' but was only a benefit to those living in faith under its provisions *prior* to knowing about the new. Indeed, it was *the* proper, divinely provided way to serve the living God in its time and was purposefully given to lead to the new.

Yet, as true as all of that is, these statements still do not address the *retrospective* question that Hebrews' own language forces us to ask, that is, whether a believer in the living God under the old covenant who has heard of and embraced the arrival of the new covenant could then go back again from the new to the old alone while *remaining* in right relation with that same living God who had now spoken climactically in and through his Son (1:2). Indeed, from the viewpoint of the author of Hebrews, such a reverse movement is certainly possible for someone to choose, which is why he warns the audience against doing it. But it is *not* possible for someone to choose this *and still be saved*, because it would mean turning back to the temporary, outward cleansing of the old as if that were sufficient unto itself rather than its being only preparatory and designed from the outset to lead towards the real substance of Christ's atoning work. In fact, given the specific design of the old and new covenants, a move from the new back to the old would necessarily involve not only a rejection of the new but also *a misunderstanding and misuse of the old itself*. It would be to choose a shadow *instead of* the true substance it figured, or in fact to treat a shadow as if it were the substance, thus rejecting the Son whom God had sent and his fully atoning blood (6:6), to which the types of the old-covenant sacrifices had pointed all along. This would entail stopping short in one's pilgrimage, refusing to go into the eschatological Canaan and the full, final rest, and opting instead for something lesser and sub-eschatological in its place.

Viewed retrospectively, then, turning to the old covenant *as an alternative to the new* would in fact be turning away from what the living God had climactically provided as the designed fulfilment of the old *and so* from the living God himself (whether one intends it this way or not) and the salvation he has provided through his Son. Yes, the old and new are both gracious and designed to serve the same ultimate outcome. Yet their respective roles in God's plan for salvation and eschatological inheritance are also decidedly different. Because of this, the former cannot function independently or as an end in itself, and to think otherwise by turning from the new to the old would have disastrous results, *even if* someone reverted to the old precisely because it was a good, God-given source of grace and atonement in its own proper time, as indeed it was.

On reflection, all of this also helps to shed light on the detail noted earlier about Hebrews 6:4–6, namely how the author does not critique the repentance that was part of the old economy, which the audience had experienced before, *and yet* still says that it is impossible to return to that repentance and receive salvific benefit from it. On the one hand, the author does not critique the first repentance, because it was the God-given gateway leading into right standing in the gracious old system, which was the greatest thing God had yet provided to his people. But on the other hand, that repentance is also impossible to return to savingly once a person has been enlightened about the coming of the new, because the good, preparatory function of the old covenant has now been fulfilled and has run its course. In addition, this explains why the author sees nothing short of judgment and destruction at stake for the audience. Because the grace *pointed towards or typified* in the old is the same grace now *present and realized* substantively in the new, any proper movement between these two systems is *one way only*. It is therefore Hebrews' own teaching about how the two covenants relate to each other that explains why something good and gracious in itself can still be impossible to return to savingly later, and why the author issues a severe warning against returning to something that it otherwise speaks so positively about in other respects.

In addition, it is precisely this relationship between shadow and true substance that also shows through in some of the author's most poignant choice of words in different warning passages. Of particular note is the vivid way he speaks in 6:6 and 10:26–29, where he characterizes the particular kind of apostasy he warns against as something that would imitate or replicate the original rejection of Christ at his crucifixion.

In 6:6, for example, the author says that being enlightened about the new covenant and then seeking to be restored to the old covenant through repentance would be tantamount to people '(re-)crucifying for themselves the Son of God and exposing him to shame'. It is important to note here how the syntax of 6:6 clearly suggests that the participles 'crucifying' and 'exposing' both modify the verb 'to be restored', not the earlier participle 'having fallen away'. First, since 'crucifying' (*anastaurountas*) and 'exposing' (*paradeigmatizontas*) are adverbial participles, they ordinarily modify the main verb in their sentence, which in this case is 'to be restored' (*anakainizein*). Second, the word order reinforces this observation, since 'crucifying' and 'exposing' both follow directly after this main verb, making it the nearest and most natural verb for those participles to modify. Third, the verb tenses reinforce the same conclusion, because 'crucifying' and 'exposing' are both in the present tense, like the verb 'to be restored', whereas the five participles in verses 4–6 that precede 'to be restored' (including the participle 'having fallen away') constitute a series of aorists. On close inspection, then, Hebrews 6:6 does not state that the general act of falling away from a Christian profession crucifies Christ and exposes him to shame. It instead says that the more particular act of being restored to repentance does this, and this makes perfect sense once the specific nature of being restored to repentance is understood as an attempt to return from the new covenant to the old, as explained above. *So, then, it is not falling away in general but the more particular act of being restored from the new covenant back to the old that resembles and so replicates the original rejection and shaming of Christ at his crucifixion.*

To similar effect in 10:26–29, the author says that rejecting the great salvation provided in the new covenant amounts to spurning the Son of God, profaning the blood of the covenant by which he was sanctified and outraging the Spirit of grace. Such concrete and historically vivid language evokes the original event of Christ's crucifixion as an occurrence in which people regarded the very sacrifice that inaugurated the new covenant as instead something common and shameful. Indeed, many of those living under the old covenant at the time had rejected Christ's sacrifice, deeming it not to be the ultimate, efficacious provision of atonement towards which the old covenant was always leading. By comparison, the author of Hebrews regards the decision facing his own audience as similar to that in its essence.[24] By choosing to go back from the new covenant to the old alone, Hebrews' audience would be attempting to live underneath the provisions of the old covenant as if it were something that did *not* find its inherent fulfilment in the Son's own person and work – a clear affront to Christ, his mediation, and the Spirit through whom he offered himself to God.

Yet, while it is necessary to describe what is at stake in Hebrews in such strong terms, in keeping with Hebrews' own language, it is also important to notice where this notion of rejecting and causing an affront to Christ fits within the author's argumentation. It is *not* described as something the audience was itself considering or intending, but just the opposite: it is described as something the author had to warn the audience about, persuading them that it would in fact be an unintended consequence of their contemplated course of action. In addition, it is introduced as a consideration that the author believed would bother his listeners and so help to *dissuade* them from that course.

On this point, it is important to note the direction of the author's argumentation in 6:1–6 and 10:19–31. He does not begin by noting the audience's objections to or low view of Christ and then seek to refute those objections in order to help them remain in the new covenant. He

[24] Others who note how apostasy in this passage entails agreeing with the original rejection of Christ at his crucifixion include Thompson (2008: 134); Schreiner (2020: 189).

instead begins by describing a course of action he wants them not to take (re-laying an old-covenant foundation in 6:1b–2, or neglecting to meet together and sinning wilfully after receiving knowledge of the truth in 10:25–26) and then moves from there to describe the consequence of that course of action (crucifying and shaming the Son of God in 6:6, or spurning the Son's blood and outraging the Spirit in 10:29) as part of the *reason* for them to avoid doing it. In this way, shaming or spurning Christ appears *not* to be how the audience itself conceived of their alternative course or to be something with which they were at all comfortable. Otherwise, there would seemingly be no benefit in the author's pointing out this consequence to them as part of his effort to dissuade them from it. As things stand, though, the author's vivid language about shaming Christ is carefully crafted to spell out the *previously unrecognized, difficult-to-stomach implications* of a course of action that the audience had themselves conceived of in a much less antithetical way.

In that sense, we could say that the minds of the audience may have been generally positive towards Christ and the new covenant, or at least not inherently critical of them. Their reasons for departing from the new covenant would therefore lie elsewhere than in a critique of it per se. It seems likely, then, that *the audience would have preferred to view the two covenants as being so similar to each other that they could be interchangeable, thus safely allowing traffic between them in either direction*. In such a situation, it makes perfect sense why the author is at pains to explain the relation between the two covenants more clearly and how they are actually historically *sequential* in their inherent design and effect, with the one pointing to, being fulfilled by, and so purposefully giving way to the other, which thereby allows only one-way movement between them.

If this inference about the intentions of Hebrews' audience is correct, we could say that this audience appears to have sought an opportunity to return to an earlier, *pre*-Christian state – the state that Moses, David and others in Hebrews 11 had inhabited prior to Christ's coming – without conceiving of that as an *anti*-Christian or Christ-dishonouring position as such. Rather than seeking something substantively different from or antithetical to the new covenant, they simply contemplated going back to a historically *prior* way of relating rightly to God through the grace and atonement that he had previously provided.

Be that as it may, when we consider the comparatively friendly and non-antithetical intentions which the audience had, the emphatic and unbending nature of the author's response stands out all the more. Despite how grace-filled the old covenant was and how noble the audience's desire to return to it may therefore have been in some respects, seeking to become *pre*-Christian again after having once been enlightened and having experienced the goodness of the new covenant is not only soterically impossible; it is also effectively *anti*-Christian in its results – *however much that may not be intended or desired in itself*. In other words, the specific problem the author sees with the temptation that faces his audience does *not* lie in the friendly or hostile nature of the audience's *intent* – how critical they were or were not seeking to be about Christ or the new covenant. It also does not lie in the degree of conflict or bitterness that was or was not present between those adhering to the new covenant and those adhering to or seeking a return to the old alone. To the contrary, as much as modern interpreters may tend to prioritize intention-based, relational or sociological concerns such as these in their religious assessments, the author of Hebrews sees the problem instead lying in the *objective* nature of the two covenants as God had originally designed them and therefore what each covenant can and cannot properly be used for in relation to God himself. So, then, it was not necessary for the audience of Hebrews to be intentionally impugning or critiquing the new covenant for them to be falling into a grave error. Conversely, it was *also* not necessary for the author of Hebrews to 'denigrate' the old covenant or 'look down' on it (which he did not do) for him to nevertheless view that covenant as temporary, preparatory, and thus unable to function independently or instead of the new. God had graciously given both covenants and designed them to function sequentially within the context of a once-for-all, irreversible historical progression between them, and to treat them differently would have disastrous effects.

By way of summary, then, in order to understand the contrast that Hebrews builds between the old and new covenants and the warnings that its author gives to the original audience, those who read this carefully crafted, nuanced sermon must keep several things in mind at the same time. First, the author clearly sees the old and new covenants in substantial continuity with each other, being based on the same promises and having the attainment of the same saving outcome and inheritance as their ultimate goal. As Patrick Gray and Amy Peeler put it: 'the new covenant – God's distinctive way of dealing with humanity through Jesus – demands the utmost allegiance and remains perfectly consistent with the divine plan as disclosed under the original covenant.'[25] Because of this, in describing the new covenant the author does not argue that Israel is rejected or replaced, much less that it never had a place among the elect (as a document such as the *Epistle of Barnabas* does).[26] Indeed, as Luke Timothy Johnson says, Hebrews 'lacks any element of supersessionism in the proper sense of the term, that is, the replacement of Israel by Gentiles as God's people'.[27] Second, the old covenant, while good and gracious, was not able to accomplish what is ultimately needed for perfection or completion and so is soterically inadequate by itself. As Craig Koester put it, the old covenant provides

> limited *means* for dealing with sin but did not bring God's purposes to completion. Therefore God made a new covenant through the death of Christ . . . providing the definitive *means* for atonement for sin, so that people might come into full and final relationship with God.[28]

Third, the new covenant is therefore a necessary, fuller development and completion of what was present in the old. As Richard Hays says in a general way, the new covenant engages with and carries forward the heritage of Israel in a way that also transforms it.[29] Or, as Paul Ellingworth explains in more detail, in the new covenant 'Christ as high priest, offering in perfect obedience to the Father the sacrifice of himself, accomplished once for all what the old priesthood and its animal sacrifices foreshadowed but could not effect'.[30] Fourth, given what has just been said, to walk away from the new covenant in favour of the old alone is therefore impossible, soteriologically speaking, and something the author strongly warns against doing. As Paul Ellingworth states, Hebrews offers both strong warning and strong encouragement 'by presenting Christ as the essential and inseparable culmination of God's purposes for his one people, under old and new dispensations alike'.[31] Because of this, 'To reject the supreme

[25] Gray and Peeler 2020: 12.

[26] See Ellingworth 1993: 24; Witherington 2007: 25; Hays 2009: 154–155.

[27] L. T. Johnson 2006: 33.

[28] Koester 2001: 110.

[29] Hays 2009: 155.

[30] Ellingworth 1993: 80.

[31] Ibid.

and final revelation of God in Christ would be to reject the living God himself: there is no alternative religion, just as there is no alternative God and no alternative salvation history'.[32] Or, as Ben Witherington notes:

> This discourse is in no way a polemic directly attacking Judaism but rather a completionist argument. It is an argument . . . that going back to non-Christian Judaism is not an option . . . any more than going forward into paganism is.[33]

Yet, in formulating such a completionist argument, Hebrews is no more anti-Jewish or supersessionist than was the community at Qumran,[34] or even an Old Testament text such as Jeremiah 31:31–34.[35]

In this way, I. Howard Marshall is correct that the relationship between the covenants is not one of good and bad but one of *historical progression*. Hebrews draws

> a contrast between the old and the new, between the partial and the perfect, and between the earthly and the heavenly . . . The contrast is not between two opposed entities but between the shadow and the reality or between the type and the antitype.

Yet, as a result of this, 'When the perfect has come, it is sin to be content with the imperfect, although the imperfect was a valid way to God before the perfect way was revealed'.[36] This is exactly why the author urges the audience towards a continuation in their pilgrimage, rather than turning back to the goodness that they themselves had probably already experienced in a firsthand way.

To illustrate with a somewhat coarse analogy from modern experience, the old covenant in Hebrews was intended to function somewhat like a jetway or airbridge at a major airport today – that moveable hallway that passengers walk on to get from their gate to the plane they wish to board. This important apparatus is designed for a very particular purpose: to connect passengers with the plane that will take them to their ultimate

[32] Ibid. 24.

[33] Witherington 2007: 26.

[34] L. T. Johnson 2006: 212.

[35] Mitchell 2007: 27.

[36] Marshall 1975: 138.

destination. As such, the jetway is a vital part of the entire transportation process. In fact, the jetway and the plane purposefully work together and are part of the same enterprise. Yet at the same time, once passengers walk across the jetway and reach their plane, the jetway itself has fulfilled its intended purpose; it begins to retract, and the plane now begins carrying them to their destination. From that point on, trying to go back to the jetway would not only be contrary to the purpose of the jetway itself but would also have a disastrous effect.

Now, to be sure, this coarse analogy is very limited in its relevance, since, among other things, the old-covenant tabernacle and sacrificial system were much more glorious, God-given and full of gracious effect than any jetway in any airport could ever be. Yet in some important respects, the design of the old covenant's ministry was still no less instrumental and temporary in its function than that: meant to help God's people for a time towards the permanent substance always designed to come in the new covenant itself, which the author and audience of Hebrews know has now arrived.

In the end, the discourse of Hebrews, as it compares and contrasts the old and new covenants, is complex and nuanced in ways that modern scholarship about old and new covenants or about Christianity and Judaism often is not. Unlike much Christian scholarship, Hebrews' discourse about these topics does not centre on a problem of either works-righteousness or ethnic exclusivism. Nor is it disparaging in its tone or content but is instead cordially appreciative of the old covenant. And yet the old covenant that it cordially appreciates has a particular design and serves a positive, preparatory purpose within God's salvific plan. As truly positive and appreciative as it is towards the old covenant, then, Hebrews nevertheless unambiguously views the old as purposefully leading to the new and therefore as something that cannot be chosen over against or in rejection of the new without rejecting the inherent value of *both* covenants. This is why it flatly insists that returning from the new covenant to the old is in fact impossible to do.

9

Situational plausibility and pastoral relevance, then and now

In the previous chapters, I have sought to make the case that, yes, the audience of Hebrews was tempted to start all over again from the ground up and that the foundation they were tempted to re-lay would be drawn from old-covenant materials alone in contrast to the new. Because of this, the author responds by arguing clearly and strongly that it is impossible to go from the new covenant back to the old alone and still be in right standing with God, since this would go against the very nature and design of both covenants. At the same time, given the nature of the issues facing the audience and the strength of the author's exhortation against returning to the old, it is all the more noticeable how positively the author speaks about the old covenant, clearly viewing it as good, gracious and purposefully preparatory to the full, final accomplishment now provided in the new.

Yet if the audience is contemplating going back to the old covenant alone, the question naturally arises why this was. What circumstances would bring this particular temptation into view or make this particular course of action seem attractive or necessary to them? This question brings us full-circle, back to the topic of the audience's larger situation, which we began discussing in chapter 1 above. While we must respect the fact that the available evidence about Hebrews' audience is sparse, as previously discussed, it can still be helpful to sketch out some historical possibilities. Doing so can at least help to show how the interpretation offered above fits plausibly with the rest of what we know about this audience. It can also provide a sense of how the author's argument was pastorally relevant for the original audience. What light does Hebrews shed, then, on why the audience may have been tempted in the way that they were?

As we set off to answer that question, though, we should also recognize that reflecting on the situation of the original audience and the relevance of Hebrews' warning for those who were in it inevitably leads to a related question regarding how Hebrews is or is not still relevant for people today, who do not live in the same kind of circumstances as the original audience did. So it is to this pair of issues regarding the relevance then and relevance now that we turn.

A plausible situation and pastoral relevance then

Naturally, we begin with the first question. If the audience of Hebrews was indeed tempted to go back and start over again with the old covenant alone, what situation or circumstances might have prompted them to consider doing this, especially after having once been enlightened about and joyfully experiencing the blessing of the new covenant?

Of course, in theory there could be many answers to that question, as other literature from the same general time period reflects. The audience could have been drawn back by the antiquity of old-covenant Jewish practice, since the antiquity of a religion was greatly valued in the ancient world.[1] They could have been struck by the fact that so many Jews and Jewish leaders had rejected Jesus as the Messiah over the course of time, leading them to lack certainty about the validity of the Christian message.[2] They could have come to see the Christian message as entailing too great a deviation in God's historic dealings with the Jewish people, which departure seemed to call God's own faithfulness and consistency into question.[3] They could have been concerned that the message of the gospel, unlike the Jewish Law, provided too small a bulwark against the kinds of immorality that were so prevalent in Gentile

[1] See, for example, how Josephus highlights the antiquity of Jewish belief and practice as a way to appeal to his contemporaries in *Ag. Ap.*, esp. 1.1–5.

[2] See, for example, the way in which Luke–Acts addresses the topic of widespread Jewish rejection in an effort to provide Theophilus with certainty (Luke 1:1–4) about the validity of the Christian movement and its message.

[3] See, for example, how Paul defends the gospel in Romans in part by emphasizing that the gospel he preaches does not involve God in being unfaithful in his dealings with the Jewish people. Rather, God has displayed his righteousness and integrity in the work of Christ and the message proclaimed about him (see Rom. 1:16–17; 3:7–8, 21–26; 9:1 – 11:36; 15:7–13).

culture.[4] They could have desired a more distinct ground for separateness and boasting through distinguishing marks such as circumcision or Law instruction.[5] Or perhaps they could have been attracted to the 'splendid ceremonial' of the Levitical sacrificial system compared to the comparatively underwhelming simplicity of the new.[6]

Yet, while all the concerns just mentioned did resonate strongly with some audiences in the first-century world, none of them resonates clearly with Hebrews' own areas of emphasis. As discussed before, Jewish social distinction from Gentiles and conflicts related to Gentile inclusion in God's people in the new-covenant period do not seem to register significantly, if at all, in Hebrews, the way they do in some other New Testament documents. Moreover, the author does not seem to consider the antiquity and venerable heritage of the old covenant as a threat to new-covenant faith or a problem to be addressed. He sees it instead as a great encouragement, since the long history of faith seen in the old-covenant period (Heb. 11) leads to and culminates in Christ himself and the faith of those in the new-covenant period, who look upward to Christ in heaven as forerunner (12:1–3). The author also does not linger over the ceremonial magnificence of the old covenant or try to respond to it, as if it were a potential stumbling block. Instead, his world view seems to naturally understand the greater value of what is invisible compared to that which is visible, a viewpoint that he does not argue for but instead simply deploys as an assumption that both he and his audience share in common. So, then, though all the reasons just mentioned have some degree of plausibility in theory, the evidence in Hebrews suggests that this audience's reasons for being attracted back to the old covenant lie elsewhere.

At this juncture, we can also note how earlier observations about the audience of Hebrews make the question of what prompted the audience to consider going back to the old covenant both more difficult and more important. In particular, it seems apparent from Hebrews' own language that the audience is not motivated by a critique of or animus against Christ and the new covenant. Instead, the author's rhetoric seems to

[4] See, for example, the concerns that some clearly had with Paul's gospel, as he acknowledges and addresses in Rom. 3:8; 6:1; and elsewhere.

[5] See, for example, the Jewish teacher's claims to superiority through Law possession and circumcision in Rom. 2:17–29, or Paul's Christian reassessment of the value of his own accomplishments prior to becoming a Christian in Phil. 3:4–9.

[6] Lindars 1991: 4.

assume that the prospect of bringing dishonour to Christ would weigh upon and even help to sway the audience away from returning to the old covenant. Far from being hardened against Christianity itself or something particular about its message, then, the audience instead remains quite sensitive to and concerned about the very topics of greatest concern to the new covenant, namely remaining in right standing with God by faith and so avoiding future judgment. Here again, the close ties between the substance of the old and new covenants, noted repeatedly above, help to cast the question we are considering in a certain light and to sharpen the nature of our enquiry. After all, if the old and new covenants are so similar, made from the same cloth, as Hebrews so repeatedly shows, then why would its audience feel the need to consider going back from the new to the old in the first place? Where does the vulnerability or liability inherent to the new covenant seem to lie, so that the audience would consider abandoning it in favour of the old?

Of course, when we begin enquiring again about the audience's broader situation, we must keep in mind what we said in chapter 1 about Hebrews' reticence to provide historical information regarding its larger context and about the tension that modern readers often experience as a result when the categories they typically emphasize in interpretation are not the kind that Hebrews itself emphasizes. As discussed before, Hebrews says precious little of a general biographical kind about its author or audience, and what it does say tends to offer very little insight into the ethnic, social and economic topics that modern readers might expect to hear about or assume are most important to contextualization.

By contrast, what the author of Hebrews *does* actually say in the course of his sermon tends to prioritize locating himself and his audience not in general historical or socio-economic terms but instead in more theologically freighted ones. This in itself is a very instructive aspect of Hebrews' thought-world to reflect upon, especially for today's readers.

For example, while we do not get much information in Hebrews that helps us to identify an absolute date for when the letter was written, the author does give significant attention to locating himself and his audience temporally. He just uses ways of identifying time periods that are different from those we are accustomed to using. In fact, the author actually begins his whole discourse by identifying the time in which he and his audience live, but he does this by sketching out different eras in which God has spoken to his people over the course of their history. Within this sketch, he specifically locates himself and his audience as living within the 'last of these days', that is, the period of time defined by the way in which God has now spoken – not just through prophets, as he did 'long ago', but specifically through his Son (1:1–2). Related to this, the author also notes later that, while he and his audience did not witness Jesus' own earthly ministry themselves, they did hear about it from those who had been eyewitnesses and 'ear-witnesses' of Jesus' preaching ministry (2:3–4).

Similarly, while we do not get enough information in Hebrews to know for sure if the author and audience were Jewish or Gentile, the author's language urging the audience not to return 'again' to the old covenant in 6:1b–2 does suggest that the audience had once experienced and lived faithfully under the provisions of the old covenant before experiencing and embracing the arrival of the new. If so, this would of course make it more likely, statistically speaking, that the audience was ethnically Jewish, as has traditionally been thought. But it also does not rule out the possibility of their having been Gentile God-fearers or proselytes,[7] and the lack of specificity in what the author says, which would otherwise illuminate this topic, is something we must respect. On balance, the author's descriptions of his audience simply focus our attention more on the audience's relation to the covenants themselves than on their membership within a specific ethnic group per se.

And again, while the language in 13:24 makes it likely that the audience (rather than the author) lived in Italy, this still does not narrow things down very much geographically (despite modern scholars' frequent insistence on pinpointing the location more specifically to Rome itself, which is mere speculation)[8] and therefore provides relatively little help with efforts at detailed historical reconstruction of the audience's specific circumstances when the author wrote. Instead, when it comes to the matter of locating his audience, the author is apparently much more interested in the fact that they assemble for worship in a *heavenly* location, Mount Zion above, where God, angels, the spirits of believers who have died and Christ himself are all located (12:22–24), than with any particular location they inhabit on earth.

[7] As Patrick Gray and Amy Peeler have said: 'Based simply on the information found in the letter, it might be difficult to distinguish a Jewish audience from an audience of Gentile God-fearers who had been socialized and instructed in a Hellenistic synagogue' (2020: 6).

[8] D. A. Carson and Douglas J. Moo (2005: 609) correctly note that identifying Rome as the audience's location, while a good guess, is still nothing more than a guess.

In these ways, we can see that Hebrews *is* in fact concerned with the time, location and circumstances of its audience, but its interest in each of these is generally defined differently and filled out with other kinds of details than those we might intuitively expect. Accordingly, we must remind ourselves again of how the specific areas of focus and the central categories of interpretation found within Hebrews' thought-world often do not fit naturally with our own, and this reminder is medicinal for interpretation if it motivates us to try to listen to Hebrews afresh on its own terms.

With that being said, though, there is one aspect of the audience's history where the author provides more information, namely about the experiences that followed their first being enlightened and entering the new covenant. Especially in 10:32–34, the author goes into uncharacteristic detail about his audience when describing the persecution that they underwent due to their original profession of faith in Christ. As described there, this persecution included public reproach and seizure of their property, as well as suffering by association with some who had been imprisoned. Then, in 12:4, the author also intimates, or at least acknowledges the real possibility, that martyrdom is something the audience could conceivably face, even if none of them had experienced it yet.[9] To be sure, the subject of martyrdom seems to constitute more of a distant threat to this audience than an imminent one, given the oblique, passing nature of the author's reference to it. But the fact that the author mentions it at all shows that the possibility of the audience's needing to resist to the point of shedding blood was not unthinkable. On reflection, while these descriptions of past and possible future persecutions still do not provide great detail, the way that they include seizure of property, imprisonment and the possibility of death for the faith does suggest that the audience faced not just persecution from unruly mobs or from zealous Jewish leaders but official opposition from somewhere within the Roman government (however sporadic it may have been), since only Rome held the authority to implement capital punishment.[10]

[9] Those viewing Heb. 12:4 as an indication of martyrdom possibly looming on the horizon for the audience include Attridge 1989: 360; Lane 1991: lxvi; Ellingworth 1993: 79. For a more extended discussion regarding the audience's situation, see also Dyer 2017; 2021.

[10] Most commentators assume that the persecution was at least partly from the Roman government. For discussion of the point, see Koester 2001: 67–69.

Yet equally important to understanding Hebrews is not just the fact that the audience had previously experienced opposition due to their Christian profession, but the fact that the author chooses to call these particular experiences to their minds at an especially climactic point in his sermon, and does so at some length. In the flow of Hebrews 10, the mention of details about past persecution is clearly meant to provide the basis for encouragement and exhortation in the audience's present. Following a lengthy discussion of the old and new covenants, which comprises the heart of the letter (7:1 – 10:18), the author gives a series of exhortations that summarize what the audience should do (10:19–25) and warns them against sinning wilfully after receiving the knowledge of the truth (10:26–31). After this, he adds a recollection of the former days of persecution in order to note the audience's exemplary response of joy at that time and so to exhort them again not to lose confidence in their Christian profession now (10:35) but to continue (10:36) without shrinking back (10:39). In this way, the author clearly recounts the audience's past experience because of the *relevance* that it has to his exhortations about their present situation. This suggests that the audience is struggling now with something sufficiently similar to what they previously experienced that they need this lengthy reminder of how well they bore up under analogous trials in the past. To be sure, this link between narration of past persecution and exhortation to present perseverance does not require that the reason for the audience's present fear must be precisely the same as it was before. Yet the amount of detail found in 10:32–34 and the uniqueness of the way the author provides it here does raise the distinct possibility that a renewal of persecution is exactly what the audience was afraid of, and the fear that it was coming again was threatening to undermine their continuing confidence as Christians.[11]

If so, then some plausible parameters for understanding the audience's situation at the time when Hebrews was written could be sketched out roughly as follows. First, given that the audience had heard the new-covenant message from eyewitnesses of Jesus' preaching and had apparently lived underneath the old covenant themselves before hearing about and

[11] Those seeing continued or renewed persecution as a major reason why Hebrews was written include Wuest 1962: 6; Marshall 1975: 137; Weeks 1977: 10; Attridge 1989: 13; Lane 1991: c–ci; L. T. Johnson 2006: 37; Mitchell 2007: 11; Witherington 2007: 28; Healy 2016: 29; Schreiner 2020: 9–10; Dyer 2017: 2. For contrasting arguments that only a general malaise or gradual loss of confidence afflicted the audience, see deSilva 2000: 18–19; Koester 2001: 71–72.

embracing the arrival of the new, a relatively early date of composition for Hebrews seems more plausible than a later one. At the very least, a date within the first century seems necessary. Second, given that the audience is exhorted to persevere in their faith largely on the basis of how the new-covenant priestly system surpasses the Levitical one, yet without the author making any mention of the destruction of the temple (either prospectively or retrospectively), a date before AD 70 does seem more likely, all things told, than one after it.[12] Third, given that the audience first experienced persecution on account of professing Christ and that this appears to have included official persecution by Rome, it stands to reason that their conversion must have happened late enough in the first century for Roman officials to have been able to distinguish Christians from non-Christian Jews, which they clearly were not able to do early on. Moreover, since it seems likely that the audience lived in Italy, this probably requires that their first experience of persecution, described in 10:32–34, occurred sometime after Claudius's expulsion of Jews from Rome (often dated to AD 49), when Roman officials appear *not* to have distinguished Christian and non-Christian Jews from one another yet.[13] At the same time, given that the audience had still not yet experienced martyrdom when Hebrews was written and that the topic of martyrdom does not seem especially urgent or emotionally distressing in the letter, but more like a distant threat, a time before Nero's persecution of Christians in AD 64 also seems more likely than any date after it.[14]

---

[12] Many who argue for a pre-70 date for Hebrews find the reference in 10:1–2 to how the Levitical offerings were made every year particularly important to their argument. After all, if the offerings had actually ceased to be offered due to the temple's destruction, would the author not have mentioned that fact to help prove old-covenant obsolescence? On reflection, the general idea that the author would likely have mentioned the temple's destruction to help prove obsolescence, if that destruction had already occurred, has some cogency to it. Regarding 10:1–2, though, it must be remembered that the author's immediate point is that the Levitical sacrifices were offered each year because they were *ineffective*. Within that particular way of arguing, a cessation of those sacrifices would thereby seem to prove their *efficacy*, which is clearly not the author's point. The author's wording in 10:1–2 therefore does not seem to prove as much as some have thought. Clearly, the sacrifices of the old covenant were offered repeatedly by design, which is the author's point, regardless of whether they were ever intermitted for other reasons, such as during the Babylonian exile.

[13] Many identify the first persecution as happening in conjunction with the Claudian expulsion of Jews in AD 49 (e.g. Bruce 1990: 270; Lane 1991: lviii; Witherington 2007: 27, 32; Thomas 2008: 119). However, Heb. 10:32–34 seems to require a situation in which Christians are already more clearly distinguished from non-Christian Jews than the situation under Claudius seems to reflect (see Isaacs 1992: 32).

[14] Alternatively, Attridge (1989: 12) and Koester (2001: 52) note that the audience of Hebrews could have belonged to a house church in Rome that did not experience the brunt of the Neronian

All told, then, dating Hebrews sometime between the mid-50s and the early 60s AD has a lot of plausibility to it, as Christians were coming to be more and more clearly distinguished from non-Christian Jews in Roman eyes in those years, leading up to the time when Nero could eventually identify Christians as a useful scapegoat for political purposes. Still, even these tentative assertions do press for more historical specificity than the available evidence allows us to claim with certainty, and so they not only remain speculative but also inevitably create the danger of allowing ourselves to replace Hebrews' native areas of primary interpretative focus with different ones of our own choosing.

Yet there is one thing that does seem certain from Hebrews, namely that the audience stands not in a position of arrogant presumption or self-importance, as was the case for some first-century Christian audiences (e.g. 1 Cor. 4:7; 5:2), but instead in a position of ongoing or renewed weakness, uncertainty and fear. And while the specific cause of this fear is not entirely certain, the presence of persecution in the past is at least *analogous* to whatever it is the audience fears now, since the author draws upon their response to those past troubles to encourage them in an ongoing way again. In addition, the effects of their current fear are clearly what creates the need for the author's repeated exhortation to continue going forward in the faith, rather than abandoning it and starting over again in the old covenant. On balance, then, hints of renewed persecution – at whatever date they may have occurred – seem to be the most likely cause of the audience's prevailing attitude of fear, in the light of which the author believed that there was an urgent need for a reminder about past confidence and an exhortation to continue in the same confession and joy that they had known before.

Yet at this juncture, the question again resurfaces about why this fearful audience, if they were going to give up on their Christian profession, would specifically be tempted to go back to the old covenant, rather than being drawn away to some alternative instead. Given the audience's history of being persecuted specifically because they embraced the new covenant (10:32–34), and given the fact that they are tempted to remedy their present fear through a return to the old covenant, it seems most likely that *a return to an old-covenant-only profession of faith appealed*

persecution, thereby making a later date still possible for Hebrews. And Thomas (2008: 120) suggests that the reference to the death of the audience's leaders in 13:7 is a reference to Paul's own death, which leads to dating Hebrews in the mid-60s.

to them especially because it offered their best possibility for greater safety while still remaining in right relation with the God of Scripture, whom they had long served. With regard to safety, returning to a more historic, old-covenant form of Jewish belief and practice would certainly give the audience a more recognized and more tolerated religious identity in Roman eyes than a specifically Christian profession did. After all, as rocky as Jewish–Roman relations were over time, the Jewish people were nevertheless a known and permissible social group (a so-called *religio licita*) as far as Rome was concerned, and the ancient pedigree of their old-covenant life and practice was something for which Romans generally had some respect. Accordingly, while factors on the ground could ebb and flow considerably in any given place and time for Jews in the Roman Empire, Rome still generally afforded the Jewish people an appreciable degree of tolerance to practise their ancestral customs. It stands to reason, then, that going backward to an earlier, old-covenant pattern of religion would garner the audience of Hebrews less negative attention in Roman eyes, thereby enabling them to avoid the kind of persecution they had undergone before, when they first became Christians.[15]

No doubt for those who have experienced persecution previously, continuing uncertainty over whether they will experience it again can have a distinct wearing effect on their outlook and sense of confidence over time. If the acute suffering they had encountered before did return, could they really endure it? And was it truly necessary to wait and find out? Was there really not any way to preclude it from happening to them again, while still remaining in right relation with God through repentance and faith?

In a vulnerable situation like this, it seems inevitable that the idea of returning to the old covenant, once it had occurred to the audience, would not only feel quite pressing existentially; its value as an escape route would also seem more and more plausible over time, holding out a unique solution to their current plight. Why not just go back to the situation they had experienced before, when they had enjoyed right relations with God through the old covenant, and so enjoy comparatively greater tolerance from Rome as well? After all, if the gracious old covenant was good enough before as a system of repentance, faith, ritual purity

---

[15] Others suggesting something similar include Marshall 1975: 137; Hughes 1977: 10; Bruce 1990: 9; Ellingworth 1993: 80; L. T. Johnson 2006: 36–37; Witherington 2007: 28; Thomas 2008: 119–120; Gray and Peeler 2020: 11: Schreiner 2020: 14–15.

(washings and laying on of hands) and future hope (resurrection and judgment), why could it not function for them that way again? Indeed, such a choice would seem especially plausible precisely when the old covenant is viewed as a system of *grace*, of the same essential substance as the new, just as Hebrews says it is. In this regard, Hebrews' clear insistence about the close, cordial relationship between the content of the old covenant and that of the new would no doubt resonate with this audience and could even seem to *support* the viability of their going back to the old system – that is, *unless* the relationship between the old and the new is precisely one of promise and fulfilment, of temporary, lesser shadow to permanent, greater substance, as the author of Hebrews is *also* at such pains to insist that it is. In that case, the older vehicle for grace cannot stand on its own as an alternative to the new, and the contours and emphases of Hebrews' argument are perfectly suited to address just this sort of question.

Now, to be sure, this sketch of the audience's situation and of Hebrews' applicability remains just one possible scenario for understanding the audience's original situation and why they were tempted to go back to the old covenant. Yet it does offer at least one example of situational plausibility within which the author's argument about historical progression between old and new covenants would not only make sense logically to his audience but would also have the pastoral relevance and urgency that his intense warnings clearly convey. More importantly to the argument of this book, the scenario sketched above also shows a plausible context within which the author's meaning would be not only quite understandable but also pointedly relevant when he insists that, for those once enlightened about the coming of the new covenant, returning in repentance and faith to right standing with God through the old alone is simply not possible.

Different situations and pastoral relevance now

Though the focus of this book has been on close investigation of the temptation that is addressed in Hebrews and the nature of the warning offered in response to that temptation, the results of the investigation also tend to broach some additional questions about the potential relevance of Hebrews' message to today's readers. In fact, at least two aspects of the results sketched out above could easily make Hebrews' applicability to audiences today seem quite minimal, at least at first glance.

First, the results sketched above place some emphasis on how little background information we have about the author and audience of Hebrews, particularly when it comes to matters such as ethnic, sexual and socio-economic factors, which are often of great importance to modern readers for conceptualizing their own situation, identity and concerns. On reflection, such a lack of information about the author and audience of Hebrews may make this sermon seem distant and impersonal to us, creating few recognizable connections between the ancient context and our own.

Second, the interpretation offered above also poses a more specific challenge to finding Hebrews relevant today due to the very specific nature of the temptation that the original audience evidently experienced, which is hardly something many could or would face in the same way today. As described above, the original audience of Hebrews had lived faithfully for some time under the old covenant, had then heard and accepted the testimony of eyewitnesses about the momentous arrival of the new covenant, and was now tempted to return to the gracious, old system of atonement they had experienced before in order to find refuge from Roman persecution. On reflection, the audience's past history, present situation and specific temptation all seem quite remote from what readers today are likely to experience. For a start, how common would it be for any community today to still be living faithfully under the provisions of the old covenant alone because they just have not yet heard of the momentous arrival of the new? Considerations like these might prompt us to question whether the interpretation offered above tends to make Hebrews so closely tied to a unique, ancient scenario that it would have little ongoing relevance today.

On further reflection, though, while the interpretation offered above may highlight certain aspects of distance between the original audience's situation and that of today's readers, it also opens up specific avenues for understanding and exploring the contemporary relevance of Hebrews. A great deal could profitably be said on this topic, but in what follows I will briefly suggest three broad areas of application for today, particularly regarding the nature of the letter's central warning, its encouragement to struggling Christians about the transcendent provisions always available to them for the sake of their perseverance, and its gracious yet uncompromising manner of arguing for its position about the uniqueness and indispensability of Christ's saving work over against any other options that a person might use for seeking right relationship with God.

First, the interpretation of Hebrews offered above sheds light, in several ways, on the continuing relevance of the warning that Hebrews issues. It has been argued above that the impossibility of returning to repentance, asserted directly in Hebrews 6 and reflected elsewhere in the letter, is not about the impossibility of returning to *Christ* after a person has apostatized. In that sense, it should be clear that Hebrews 6:4–6 is not an 'unforgivable sin' text, stating that a certain sin or certain type of apostasy cannot be forgiven later by turning back to Christ in faith.[16] Instead, Hebrews' warning concerns the impossibility of returning to right standing in *the old covenant* after having heard of and embraced the new. To be clear, Hebrews does support saying that a person who rejects Christ himself lacks proper mediation before God and so should expect his judgment, unless they have a change of heart and return to Christ again. But it is important to emphasize that Hebrews does not say that a person who rejects Christ once is therefore barred from ever returning to him thereafter for forgiveness, as some have mistakenly thought.

Along with this, the interpretation above helps to show how the apostasy that Hebrews speaks of and the warning that it issues are not merely hypothetical but quite real. After all, it is not a mere theoretical possibility, whether in the first century or now, that a member of the new-covenant community who has professed faith in Christ and participated in the church's blessings and fellowship could later be drawn away into a non-Christian Jewish profession of faith instead. In this respect, both the attraction of the old covenant and the difficulty of persecution for professing Christ were very real in that context, and both those and other potential reasons for leaving behind one's Christian profession also confront people today.

In fact, while it is beyond the scope of the present book to explore it fully, other parts of the New Testament certainly describe a range of

[16] Regarding the notion of a sin or sins that cannot be forgiven, see esp. Luke 12:10 and parallels, where Jesus states that, while those who speak against the Son of Man will be forgiven, those who speak against the Holy Spirit will not. For helpful analysis, see Bock 1996: 2: 1141–1143. Also note 1 John 5:16, which mentions a 'sin unto death' and says that, unlike when praying for a fellow brother or sister in the faith, believers are not able to have confidence that those committing this sin will in fact be forgiven. For helpful analysis of what 1 John 5:16 does and does not mean, see Yarbrough 2008: 309–310. See also Jobes 2014: 236.

reasons why a brother or sister in Christ might eventually fall away, against which temptations Christians must always be on guard. For example, Jesus' teaching in Mark 4:16–19 shows that a person who receives the word of God, responds joyfully to it and grows on account of it could still end up not continuing in their faith due to such things as persecution, the cares of this world or the deceitfulness of wealth, and so fall away and receive judgment. Similarly, Paul teaches that it is those who think they stand firm who must take heed in order not to fall (1 Cor. 10:12) and that even the one who is spiritual must be careful not to be tempted (Gal. 6:1). So, then, it is not just Hebrews that warns about real dangers posed by real temptations to fall away.

Now, to be sure, 1 John 2:19 suggests that a member of the community who has apostatized has thereby made it clear after the fact that he or she was not truly 'of us', that is, that they were not born from God (2:29) or, as we might say, not truly regenerate. And teachings elsewhere about God's electing love and his infallible purpose and ability to preserve his children also provide strong and needed encouragement for those placing their confidence in Christ: that nothing whatsoever can separate those elected by God from his saving love (Rom. 8:30, 35, 39), that Christ will not lose one of those whom the Father has given him but will raise them up at the last day (John 6:39–40) and that the one who began a good work in believers will in fact be faithful to bring that work to completion at the day of Christ (Phil. 1:6).

Nevertheless, while the range of biblical teachings about God's preservation of his people and their security in Christ can and should be carefully considered in order to do justice to these larger topics (something that lies beyond the scope of this book), the warning of Hebrews must also be taken with full seriousness. If it is true, sadly, that some members of the new-covenant community do eventually show that they are not actually 'of us' by apostatizing, Hebrews sounds a very real and needed alarm, which is by no means merely theoretical. And in so doing, the author depicts some of the real challenges of life as a Christian and something of the pastoral approach that is needed towards those in the church. As Hebrews shows, Christians facing pressures to apostatize need to understand how other supposed sources of confidence before God besides Christ are ultimately futile, to appreciate the magnitude and sufficiency of the work of Christ to give confident access to God's presence and mercy, to be urged to continue in their profession of faith in Christ despite difficulty and fear, and to be warned in all sincerity about the dire consequences of growing weary and giving up.

On this score, while it could be easy to think that the very specific nature of the apostasy that Hebrews warns against would greatly limit the relevance of its warnings for people today, this is not actually the case. Certainly, Hebrews' warning is deeply embedded in a specific sort of first-century context that people in our time do not face in the same way. Nevertheless, what the author says in response to that situation still has strong implications today. Of particular importance here is an a fortiori argument that can readily be derived from what the author of Hebrews says to his own audience about the person and work of Christ. After all, if the new-covenant work of Christ fulfils and brings to completion what the old covenant itself had provided, such that, as good and gracious as the old covenant was, it was *still* not sufficient for salvation either apart from or as a replacement for Christ, then *how much more* is any other, qualitatively lesser source of confidence and blessing also insufficient for that purpose? In particular, where else could one conceivably go to properly deal with sin, cleanse the conscience and provide necessary advocacy before God's throne of judgment in heaven, other than to Christ? In other words, *if even the very best thing that God had ever provided throughout all of history prior to the coming of Christ – namely the old covenant with its priests, sacrifices, place of holiness, and angelic mediation – was not sufficient in itself to provide salvation and would only bring judgment if used as a replacement for Christ, then what else could any of us today successfully appeal to as an alternative to Christ*? Given how Hebrews describes the sole sufficiency of the new-covenant blessings in Christ, the answer is very clear.

Here again, the deep appreciation and respect that the author of Hebrews holds for the old covenant is on display, and this is what makes the above logical implication of his argument especially pointed and instructive for us. Indeed, it is precisely because he does *not* disparage the old covenant or call it ungracious but instead admires and draws much positive material from it and from the experience of believers under it and yet *still* sees it as ultimately insufficient for salvation that the logic of his argument has such strong implications regarding any other religion, philosophy or world view that might be advocated more commonly today as an alternative source of hope to the Christian one. After all, it is not something paltry or meagre that the author says cannot operate as an alternative to Christ; it is something exceedingly substantive and admirable. Put differently, the author's persistent argument from good (old covenant) to better (new covenant) readily supports a parallel conclusion that all other things besides the God-given, gracious, old-covenant forms of blood atonement are even *less* sufficient on their own to provide salvation, whatever it is that we today may be tempted to try to base our lives on instead. In this way, though our specific situation may be quite different from the one that Hebrews' audience faced, and the particular form of temptation to fall away from Christ might be quite different from what Hebrews directly addressed, we can still find the author's argument quite searching and convicting, given the supreme and sole position that he sees Christ occupying within the whole scope of God's redemptive plan and provision.

Second, it has been noted repeatedly above how relatively hidden the author and audience of Hebrews are within the pages of the letter. Hebrews says something about each, to be sure, but not very much, especially within the scope of such a long document. In itself, Hebrews' characteristic reticence may seem to make it obscure and unrelatable to us today. But without diminishing the value of efforts to reconstruct historical context where possible – indeed, I would be thrilled to know more details about Hebrews' author and audience through any legitimate means available to us – something else should also be observed here. In point of fact, it is often *because* the author does not focus on ordinary sociocultural details about himself or his audience, but instead locates himself and them primarily in relation to transcendent, theological realities of a very different sort, that the instruction and encouragement he provides is still so abidingly relevant to Christians living at all times and in all situations, including today. After all, whether the audience of Hebrews was predominantly composed of Jewish Christians tempted to go back to Judaism in the mid-first century, as many have traditionally thought, or Gentile Christians discouraged by the destruction of the temple in the late first or early second century, as some revisionists have more recently suggested, neither of these scenarios actually creates a high degree of sociocultural similarity with or connection to the situation of most people today. In fact, in either such scenario, knowing more about and focusing on the socio-historical situation of author and audience actually creates considerable cognitive distance between us and them instead.

However, if the audience is to be located in the 'last of these days' when God has spoken in his Son (1:2) and in a day when the promise of entering a future, eternal sabbath rest still stands (4:1, 9), and if the audience assembles by faith at the heavenly Mount Zion where the risen Christ continually intercedes on the basis of his once-for-all sacrifice as part of a ministry that is the same yesterday, today and for ever (12:22–24; 13:8), then it more readily becomes clear how Christians today actually share the same essential time and location as the audience of Hebrews itself, at least as the author has defined them, and so are able to enjoy the same essential *benefits* flowing from one and the same abiding redemptive provision as they did. On further reflection, then, the focus that Hebrews has – not so much on the social and cultural categories that often preoccupy modern scholarship, but more on abiding realities that transcend differences of time and space – actually serves to make its argument and its rationale much more readily *applicable* to people today than it would otherwise have been.

In a sense, then, part of what makes Hebrews less relatable to us when we focus on sociocultural elements of our experience also makes it ongoingly *relevant* to us at an even deeper level, which we would often do well to think about more anyway. In fact, this observation might even encourage us to pause and reflect on whether sociocultural ways of understanding and identifying ourselves are really the *deepest* and most abidingly important ones for us to focus on for our own self-understanding. At least for its part, Hebrews seems preoccupied with more fundamental structures of reality, such as the abiding difference between body and soul, earth and heaven, or the temporary and the eternal, as well as with the reality-defining results of God's own actions in the last of these days in and through his Son to redeem a people for himself – concerns that transcend but are nevertheless quite relevant to people living within each individual time and place, both then and now.

To be clear, I am *not* arguing that Hebrews turns away from having concern for ordinary elements of life on this earth in favour of something abstract and unrelated to history, earthly cultures or individual situations. Instead, Hebrews focuses its attention on abiding, culture-transcending categories and topics in a way that actually has significant, even direct *ramifications* for life in any earthly time, place or culture, including our own. In fact, we should be quick to note in this regard that, even while Hebrews prefers to locate its audience, their concerns and its message in relation to God's own speech and acts and other transcendent and heavenly realities rather than focusing on temporary, socio-economic or political concerns, at the same time this very theologically rich way of locating our lives does not conflict with or deny but instead helps *support and direct* practical concern for how to live life in the here and now, both individually and corporately. Some of the practical concern expressed in the letter relates to such religious topics as how people should approach God's throne with confidence in worship and prayer through Christ's mediation (10:22). Yet other exhortations have more ordinary, sublunary and social dimensions to them too, such as that the audience should continue meeting together regularly in the Christian assembly (10:25) and exhorting one another daily towards perseverance (3:13). Also included are direct exhortations to provide hospitality to strangers (13:2), to identify with and care for the needy and marginalized (13:3, 16), to maintain ethical purity in general and sexual purity in the sanctity of the marriage bed in particular (13:4–6), and to remember and follow the example of godly communal leaders past and present (13:7, 17). Each of these exhortations and others like them involve living out and giving practical, outward expression to the heavenly, transcendently defined identity that the letter inculcates within its readers, rather than encouraging any sort of bloodless, abstract indifference towards social and ethical life here and now.

In other words, while Hebrews provides a perspective that focuses on transcendent, theological realities rather than immanently economic, sexual or political ones, it also strongly emphasizes living out that transcendent perspective in practical and socially significant ways. In that sense, the heavenly-mindedness displayed in Hebrews is not something that produces flight from and uselessness in the world. If anything, the security and confidence that Hebrews' broad, transcendent perspective on life provides, as we look ultimately to an inheritance in a heavenly city rather than any earthly one (13:14), should instead produce a mindset that gives *greater freedom for and endurance in concrete acts of service to others* in the details of daily life, no matter what particular time, place or situation one inhabits and experiences.[17] In these ways, the relative paucity of detailed historical information that this anonymous sermon

[17] For salutary reflections on this theme in Hebrews, including as it relates to Christian involvement in general cultural endeavours in this age, see Vos 1994.

provides can actually serve indirectly to enhance its relevance to us by turning our attention to an abiding, eternal provision that continually guides and enables a rich Christian practice in every situation here below.

Finally, another aspect of Hebrews' argument that has been noted repeatedly above is how positive it is about the nature and substance of the old covenant, even though it is the old covenant itself that, in certain respects, constitutes a 'threat' to the ongoing spiritual health of the audience. In this respect, Hebrews shows itself to be remarkably non-reactionary and non-reductionistic when discussing the very thing that in some ways it is arguing 'against', and this very fact provides us with a great example of religious and theological discourse that is balanced, fair-minded and not unnecessarily polemical. After all, while Hebrews speaks quite positively about the old covenant, it also does not pull punches when it comes to describing the great differences between the old and the new and the impossibility of going back from the one to the other. In this way, Hebrews is not only quite nuanced in what it says about the old covenant but also quite clear about its own soteriological convictions, refusing to shy away from the ultimate and exclusive claims of Christ that it so strongly believes in and the clear deliberative implications that that has for the audience's own decision-making.

So, then, the discourse found in Hebrews avoids, on the one hand, any kind of one-sided, tendentious, reductionistic argumentation that would cause reactionary polarization, and, on the other hand, a tendency towards unclarity, concessiveness or compromise that would obscure the distinctive claims inherent to the very nature of Christ's cross and ascension. Happily, therefore, the author of Hebrews does not feel the need to disparage the old covenant in order to exalt the new. Neither does he settle for the blithe conclusion that the two are ultimately interchangeable, given the obvious similarities that they do indeed share. He instead carves out a more nuanced and complex space and in so doing sets an example to all of us regarding theological discourse – offering at one and the same time both genuine, substantive appreciation of the old covenant and a genuine, robust warning about its potential misuse and the life-or-death, salvation-or-judgment consequences entailed in that.

This, it seems to me, is one more way that Hebrews remains profitable and relevant today. In an era in which reductionism, invective and dismissal of others' positions abound in some theological circles, while vagueness, ungrounded concession, and compromise about the theological substance and distinctives of the Christian faith abound in others, Hebrews has much to teach us all, not only by *what* it says but also by *how* it says it. And this dual character of its discourse – as both balanced and uncompromising – is even more readily seen and appreciated when the precise kind of temptation the audience faces (a desire to return to the old covenant alone), the particular kind of warning that the author issues (that returning to the old is salvifically impossible) and the particular rationale he uses for this warning (that the good, gracious old is fundamentally preparatory and cannot be used as an alternative to the better, gracious new) are each understood in the way argued for above.

With an unusually non-reductionistic, non-reactionary way of speaking, the author of Hebrews nevertheless issues a clear, unflinching and pastorally calibrated message offering both strong warning and great hope. Throughout its pages, this magisterial letter-sermon therefore provides much that is relevant and instructive for God's people, both in the ancient world and today. So, as we read and reflect on it, may we too be among those who listen attentively, receive it sensitively, and profit from it by faith, both now and as we move into the economy of the great heavenly city (13:14) and the future inhabited world still to come (2:5).

Bibliography

Adams, J. C. (1967), 'Exegesis of Hebrews VI.1f.', *NTS* 13: 378–385.

Alexander, L. (2009), 'Prophets and Martyrs as Exemplars of Faith', in Richard Bauckham, Daniel R. Driver, Trevor A. Hart and Nathan MacDonald (eds.), *The Epistle to the Hebrews and Christian Theology*, Grand Rapids: Eerdmans, 405–421.

Attridge, H. W. (1989), *The Epistle to the Hebrews: A Commentary on the Epistle to the Hebrews*, Hermeneia, Philadelphia: Fortress.

—— (1990), 'Paraenesis in a Homily (λόγος παρακλήσεως): The Possible Location of, and Socialization in, the "Epistle to the Hebrews"', *Semeia* 50: 211–226.

Barclay, M. G. (2015), *Paul and the Gift*, Grand Rapids: Eerdmans.

Barrett, C. K. (1964), 'The Eschatology of the Epistle to the Hebrews', in W. D. Davies and D. Daube (eds.), *The Background of the New Testament and Its Eschatology: Studies in Honour of C. H. Dodd*, Cambridge: Cambridge University Press, 363–393.

Bassler, J. M. (1996), *1 Timothy, 2 Timothy, Titus*, ANTC, Nashville: Abingdon, 1996.

Bateman IV, H. W. (ed.) (2007), *Four Views on the Warning Passages in Hebrews*, Grand Rapids: Kregel.

Behm, J., and E. Würthwein (1964–76), 'μετανόεω κ.τ.λ.', *TDNT*, 4: 975–1008.

Bock, D. L. (1996), *Luke*, 2 vols., BECNT, Grand Rapids: Baker Academic.

Boda, M. J. (2015), *'Return to Me': A Biblical Theology of Repentance*, NSBT 3, London: Apollos; Downers Grove: InterVarsity Press.

Bruce, F. F. (1990), *The Epistle to the Hebrews*, rev. edn, NICNT, Grand Rapids: Eerdmans.

Cara, R. J. (2024), *Hebrews*, Mentor, Fearn: Christian Focus.

Carson, D. A., and D. J. Moo (2005), *An Introduction to the New Testament*, 2nd edn, Grand Rapids: Zondervan.

Cockerill, G. L. (2007), 'A Wesleyan Arminian View', in Herbert W. Bateman IV (ed.), *Four Views on the Warning Passages in Hebrews*, Grand Rapids: Kregel, 2007, 257–292.

deSilva, D. A. (2000), *Perseverance in Gratitude: A Socio-Rhetorical Commentary on the Epistle 'to the Hebrews'*, Grand Rapids: Eerdmans.

Dyer, B. R. (2017), *Suffering in the Face of Death: The Epistle to the Hebrews and Its Context of Situation*, LNTS 568, London: Bloomsbury.

—— (2021), '"All of These Died in Faith": Hebrews 11 and Faith in the Face of Death', *CBQ* 83.4: 638–654.

Easter, M. C. (2024), '"Profane Like Esau": Sexual Immorality, Bitterness, and Community Abandonment in Hebrews 12:14–17', *NovT* 66: 112–125.

Eisenbaum, P. M. (2005a), 'Hebrews, Supersessionism and Jewish-Christian Relations', paper delivered at SBL Annual Meeting Hebrews Consultation, Philadelphia, 1–6.

—— (2005b), 'Locating Hebrews within the Literary Landscape of Christian Origins', in Gabriella Gelardini (ed.), *Hebrews: Contemporary Methods — New Insights*, Boston: Brill, 213–237.

Ellingworth, P. (1993), *The Epistle to the Hebrews: A Commentary on the Greek Text*, NIGTC, Grand Rapids: Eerdmans.

Emmrich, M. (2003), 'Hebrews 6:4–6 – Again! (A Pneumatological Inquiry)', *WTJ* 65.1: 83–95.

Fanning, B. M. (2007), 'A Classical Reformed View', in Herbert W. Bateman IV (ed.), *Four Views on the Warning Passages in Hebrews*, Grand Rapids: Kregel, 172–219.

Gaffin Jr, R. B. (1987), *Resurrection and Redemption: A Study in Paul's Soteriology*, Phillipsburg: P&R.

Gelardini, G. (2005), 'Hebrews, an Ancient Synagogue Homily for Tisha be-Av: Its Function, Its Basis, Its Theological Interpretation', in Gabriella Gelardini (ed.), *Hebrews: Contemporary Methods – New Insights*, Boston: Brill, 107–127.

Gleason, R. C. (2007), 'A Moderate Reformed View', in Herbert W. Bateman IV (ed.), *Four Views on the Warning Passages in Hebrews*, Grand Rapids: Kregel, 336–377.

Gordon, R. P. (2008), *Hebrews*, 2nd edn, Sheffield: Sheffield Phoenix Press.

Gray, P. (2011), 'Hebrews among Greeks and Romans', in Eric F. Mason and Kevin B. McCruden (eds.), *Reading the Epistle to the Hebrews: A Resource for Students*, Atlanta: SBL, 13–30.

Gray, P., and A. Peeler (2020), *Hebrews: An Introduction and Study Guide*, London: T&T Clark.

Grindheim, S. (2023), *The Letter to the Hebrews*, PNTC, Grand Rapids: Eerdmans.

Grudem, W. (2000), 'Perseverance of the Saints: A Case Study from the Warning Passages of Hebrews', in T. R. Schreiner and B. A. Ware (ed.), *Still Sovereign: Contemporary Perspectives on Election, Foreknowledge, and Grace*, Grand Rapids: Baker, 133–182.

Hays, R. B. (2009), '"Here We Have No Lasting City": New Covenantalism in Hebrews', in Richard Bauckham, Daniel R. Driver, Trevor A. Hart and Nathan MacDonald (eds.), *The Epistle to the Hebrews in Christian Theology*, Grand Rapids: Eerdmans, 151–173.

Healy, M. (2016), *Hebrews*, CCSS, Grand Rapids: Baker Academic.

Hooker, M. D. (2009), 'Christ, the "End" of the Cult', in Richard Bauckham, Daniel R. Driver, Trevor A. Hart and Nathan MacDonald (eds.), *The Epistle to the Hebrews in Christian Theology*, Grand Rapids: Eerdmans, 189–212.

Hughes, P. E. (1977), *A Commentary on the Epistle to the Hebrews*, Grand Rapids: Eerdmans.

Isaacs, M. (1992), *Sacred Space: An Approach to the Theology of Hebrews*, JSNTSup 73, Sheffield: Sheffield Academic Press.

Jamieson, R. B. (2021), *The Paradox of Sonship: Christology in the Epistle to the Hebrews*, SCDS, Downers Grove: IVP Academic; London: Apollos.

Jobes, K. H. (2014), *1, 2, & 3 John*, ZECNT, Grand Rapids: Zondervan Academic.

Johnson, D. E. (2007), 'The Epistle to the Hebrews as an Apostolic Preaching Paradigm', in *Him We Proclaim: Preaching Christ from All the Scriptures*, Phillipsburg: P&R, 167–197.

—— (2018), *Hebrews*, ESV Expository Commentary, vol. 12, Wheaton: Crossway.

Johnson, L. T. (1999), *The Writings of the New Testament*, Minneapolis: Fortress.

—— (2006), *Hebrews: A Commentary*, NTL, Louisville: Westminster John Knox.

Knight III, G. W. (1992), *The Pastoral Epistles: A Commentary on the Greek Text*, NIGTC, Grand Rapids: Eerdmans.

Koester, C.R. (2001), *Hebrews: A New Translation with Introduction and Commentary*, AB 36, New York: Doubleday.

Lane, W. L. (1991), *Hebrews 1–8*, WBC 47A, Dallas: Word.

Lindars, B. (1991), *The Theology of the Epistle to the Hebrews*, Cambridge: Cambridge University Press.

Löhr, H. (1994), *Umkehr und Sünde im Hebräerbrief*, BZNW 73, New York: De Gruyter.

McKnight, S. (1992), 'The Warning Passages of Hebrews: A Formal Analysis and Theological Conclusions', *TrinJ* 13.1: 21–59.

Marshall, I. H. (1975), *Kept by the Power of God: A Study of Perseverance and Falling Away*, Minneapolis: Bethany Fellowship.

Martin, M. W., and J. A. Whitlark (2023), 'Strengthened by Grace and Not by Foods: Reconsidering the Literary, Theological, and Social Context of Hebrews 13:7–14', *NovT* 65: 350–380.

—— (2024), 'The Lord's Altar as an Alternative Food Source in Hebrews 13:9–10', *CBQ* 86: 348–368.

Mason, F. (2010), 'The Epistle (Not Necessarily) to the "Hebrews": A Call to Renunciation of Judaism or Encouragement to Christian Commitment?' *Perspectives on Religious Studies* 37.1: 7–20.

Mathewson, D. (1999), 'Reading Heb 6:4–6 in Light of the Old Testament', *WTJ* 61.2: 209–225.

Metzger, B. M. (2006), *A Textual Commentary on the Greek New Testament: A Companion Volume to the United Bible Societies' Greek New Testament*, 2nd edn, Peabody: Hendrickson.

Michel, O. (1975), *Der Brief an die Hebräer*, KEK 13, Göttingen: Vandenhoeck & Ruprecht.

Mitchell, A. C. (2007), *Hebrews*, SP 13, Collegeville: Liturgical Press.

—— (2011), '"A Sacrifice of Praise": Does Hebrews Promote Supersessionism?' in Eric F. Mason and Kevin B. McCruden (eds.), *Reading the Epistle to the Hebrews: A Resource for Students*, Atlanta: SBL, 251–268.

Moffitt, D. M. (2011), *Atonement and the Logic of Resurrection in the Epistle to the Hebrews*, NovTSup 141, Boston: Brill.

—— (2012), 'Blood, Life, and Atonement: Reassessing Hebrews' Christological Appropriation of Yom Kippur', in *The Day of Atonement: Its Interpretations in Early Jewish and Christian Traditions*, Boston: Brill, 211–224.

—— (2016), 'The Role of Jesus' Resurrection in the Epistle to the Hebrews, Once Again: A Brief Response to Jean-René Moret', *NTS* 62.2: 308–314.

—— (2021), 'Jesus' Sacrifice and the Mosaic Logic of Hebrews' New-Covenant Theology', in Gerald R. McDermott (ed.), *Understanding the Jewish Roots of Christianity: Biblical, Theological, and Historical Essays on the Relationship between Christianity and Judaism*, Bellingham: Lexham Press, 51–68.

Montague, G. T. (2008), *First and Second Timothy, Titus*, CCSS, Grand Rapids: Baker Academic.

Nicole, R. (1975), 'Some Comments on Hebrews 6:4–6 and the Doctrine of the Perseverance of God with the Saints', in G. F. Hawthorne (ed.), *Current Issues in Biblical and Patristic Interpretation: Studies in Honor of Merrill C. Tenney*, Grand Rapids: Eerdmans, 355–364.

Oberholtzer, T. K. (1988), 'The Thorn-Infested Ground in Hebrews 6:4–12', *BSac* 145: 319–328.

Oldfather, W. A. (tr.) (1998), *Epictetus: The Discourses as Reported by Arrian, Books I–II*, Cambridge: Harvard University Press.

Oropeza, B. J. (2011), 'The Warning Passages in Hebrews: Revised Theologies and New Methods of Interpretation', *CBR* 10.1: 81–100.

Osborne, G. R. (2007), 'A Classical Arminian View', in Herbert W. Bateman IV (ed.), *Four Views on the Warning Passages in Hebrews*, Grand Rapids: Kregel, 86–128.

Owen, H. P. (1956–57), 'The "Stages of Ascent" in Hebrews V.11–VI.3', *NTS* 3: 243–253.

Peeler, A. L. (2014), *You Are My Son: The Family of God in the Epistle to the Hebrews*, LNTS, New York: Bloomsbury.

Penniman, J. D. (2017), *Raised on Christian Milk: Food and the Formation of the Soul in Early Christianity*, Synkrisis, New Haven: Yale University Press.

Peterson, D. G. (2020), *Hebrews: An Introduction and Commentary*, TNTC 15, London: Inter-Varsity Press; Downers Grove: IVP Academic.

Salevao, I. (2002), *Legitimation in the Letter to the Hebrews: The Construction and Maintenance of a Symbolic Universe*, JSNTSup 219, Sheffield: Sheffield Academic Press.

Schenck, K. (2003), *Understanding the Book of Hebrews: The Story behind the Story*, Louisville: Westminster John Knox.

—— (2007), *Cosmology and Eschatology in Hebrews: The Settings of the Sacrifice*, SNTSMS 143, Cambridge: Cambridge University Press.

—— (2011), 'Hebrews as the Re-presentation of a Story: A Narrative Approach to Hebrews', in Eric F. Mason and Kevin B. McCruden (eds.), *Reading the Epistle to the Hebrews: A Resource for Students*, Atlanta: SBL, 171–188.

—— (2019), *A New Perspective on Hebrews: Rethinking the Parting of the Ways*, Lanham: Fortress Academic.

Schmidt, K. L. (1964–76), 'θεμέλιος κ.τ.λ.', *TDNT*, 3: 63–64.

Schnackenburg, R. (1950), 'Typen der Metanoia-Predigt im Neuen Testament', *MThZ* 1.4: 1–13.

Schreiner, T. (2015), *Commentary on Hebrews*, Biblical Theology for Christian Proclamation, Nashville: B&H.

—— (2020), *Hebrews*, EBib, Bellingham: Lexham Academic.

Silva, M. (ed.) (2014), 'μετανοέω κ.τ.λ.', *NIDNTTE*, 3: 290–293.

Solari, J. K. (1970), 'The Problem of *Metanoia* in the Epistle to the Hebrews', PhD diss., Catholic University of America.

Spicq, C. (1952), *L'Épître aux Hébreux*, 2 vols., EBib, Paris: Gabalda.

Stedman, R. C. (2009), *Hebrews*, IVPNTC, Downers Grove: InterVarsity Press.

Thomas, C. A. (2008), *A Case for Mixed-Audience with Reference to the Warning Passages in the Book of Hebrews*, New York: Peter Lang.

Thompson, J. (1982), *The Beginnings of Christian Philosophy: The Epistle to the Hebrews*, CBQMS 13, Washington: Catholic Biblical Association of America.

—— (2008), *Hebrews*, Paideia, Grand Rapids: Baker Academic.

—— (2011), 'What Has Middle Platonism to Do with Hebrews?' in Eric F. Mason and Kevin B. McCruden (eds.), *Reading the Epistle to the Hebrews: A Resource for Students*, Atlanta: SBL, 31–52.

Thyen, H. (1955), *Der Stil der jüdisch-hellenistichen Homilie*, FRLANT 47, Göttingen: Vandenhoeck & Ruprecht.

Towner, P. H. (2006), *The Letters to Timothy and Titus*, NICNT, Grand Rapids: Eerdmans.

Verbrugge, V. D. (1980), 'Towards a New Interpretation of Hebrews 6:4–6', *CTJ* 15: 61–73.

Vos, G. (1956), *The Teaching of the Epistle to the Hebrews*, ed. Johannes G. Vos, Grand Rapids: Eerdmans.

—— (1994), 'Heavenly-Mindedness', in *Grace and Glory: Sermons Preached in the Chapel of Princeton Theological Seminary*, Carlisle: Banner of Truth Trust, 103–123.

Watson, F. (2007), *Paul, Judaism, and the Gentiles*, rev. and exp. edn, Grand Rapids: Eerdmans.

Weeks, N. (1976), 'Admonition and Error in Hebrews', *WTJ* 39: 72–80.

Weiss, H.-F. (1991), *Der Brief an die Hebräer*, KEK 15, Göttingen: Vandenhoeck & Ruprecht.

Westerholm, S. (2004), *Perspectives Old and New on Paul: The 'Lutheran' Paul and His Critics*, Grand Rapids: Eerdmans.

Whiston, W. (tr.) (1895), *The Works of Flavius Josephus*, 4 vols., Buffalo: John E. Beardsley.

Whitlark, J. A. (2014), *Resisting Empire: Rethinking the Purpose of the 'Letter to the Hebrews'*, LNTS 484, London: T&T Clark.

Wills, L. (1984), 'The Form of the Sermon in Hellenistic Judaism and Early Christianity', *HTR* 77: 277–299.

Witherington III, B. C. (2006), *Letters and Homilies for Hellenized Christians, vol. 1: A Socio-Rhetorical Commentary on Titus, 1–2 Timothy, and 1–3 John*, Downers Grove: IVP Academic.

—— (2007), *Letters and Homilies for Jewish Christians: A Socio-Rhetorical Commentary on Hebrews, James and Jude*, Downers Grove: IVP Academic.

Wuest, K. S. (1962), 'Hebrews Six in the Greek New Testament', *BSac* 119.473: 45–53, <www.galaxie.com/article/bsac119-473-06> (accessed 10 December 2024).

Yarbrough, B. (2008), *1–3 John*, BECNT, Grand Rapids: Baker Academic.

Yinger, K. L. (2011), *The New Perspective on Paul: An Introduction*, Eugene: Cascade.

Yonge, C. D. (tr.) (1993), *The Works of Philo: Complete and Unabridged*, new and updated edn, Peabody: Hendrickson.

Index of authors

Index of Scripture references

James

1 Peter

2 Peter

Jude

Revelation

Titles in this series:

1 *Possessed by God*, David Peterson
2 *God's Unfaithful Wife*, Raymond C. Ortlund Jr
3 *Jesus and the Logic of History*, Paul W. Barnett
4 *Hear, My Son*, Daniel J. Estes
5 *Original Sin*, Henri Blocher
6 *Now Choose Life*, J. Gary Millar
7 *Neither Poverty Nor Riches*, Craig L. Blomberg
8 *Slave of Christ*, Murray J. Harris
9 *Christ, Our Righteousness*, Mark A. Seifrid
10 *Five Festal Garments*, Barry G. Webb
12 *Now My Eyes Have Seen You*, Robert S. Fyall
13 *Thanksgiving*, David W. Pao
14 *From Every People and Nation*, J. Daniel Hays
15 *Dominion and Dynasty*, Stephen G. Dempster
16 *Hearing God's Words*, Peter Adam
17 *The Temple and the Church's Mission*, G. K. Beale
18 *The Cross from a Distance*, Peter G. Bolt
19 *Contagious Holiness*, Craig L. Blomberg
20 *Shepherds After My Own Heart*, Timothy S. Laniak
21 *A Clear and Present Word*, Mark D. Thompson
22 *Adopted into God's Family*, Trevor J. Burke
23 *Sealed with an Oath*, Paul R. Williamson
24 *Father, Son and Spirit*, Andreas J. Köstenberger and Scott R. Swain
25 *God the Peacemaker*, Graham A. Cole
26 *A Gracious and Compassionate God*, Daniel C. Timmer
27 *The Acts of the Risen Lord Jesus*, Alan J. Thompson
28 *The God Who Makes Himself Known*, W. Ross Blackburn
29 *A Mouth Full of Fire*, Andrew G. Shead
30 *The God Who Became Human*, Graham A. Cole
31 *Paul and the Law*, Brian S. Rosner
32 *With the Clouds of Heaven*, James M. Hamilton Jr
33 *Covenant and Commandment*, Bradley G. Green
34 *Bound for the Promised Land*, Oren R. Martin
35 *'Return to Me'*, Mark J. Boda
36 *Identity and Idolatry*, Richard Lints
37 *Who Shall Ascend the Mountain of the Lord?*, L. Michael Morales

38 *Calling on the Name of the Lord*, J. Gary Millar
40 *The Book of Isaiah and God's Kingdom*, Andrew T. Abernethy
41 *Unceasing Kindness*, Peter H. W. Lau and Gregory Goswell
42 *Preaching in the New Testament*, Jonathan I. Griffiths
43 *God's Mediators*, Andrew S. Malone
44 *Death and the Afterlife*, Paul R. Williamson
45 *Righteous by Promise*, Karl Deenick
46 *Finding Favour in the Sight of God*, Richard P. Belcher Jr
47 *Exalted Above the Heavens*, Peter C. Orr
48 *All Things New*, Brian J. Tabb
49 *The Feasts of Repentance*, Michael J. Ovey
50 *Including the Stranger*, David G. Firth
51 *Canon, Covenant and Christology*, Matthew Barrett
52 *Biblical Theology According to the Apostles*, Chris Bruno, Jared Compton and Kevin McFadden
53 *Salvation to the Ends of the Earth (2nd edn)*, Andreas J. Köstenberger with T. Desmond Alexander
54 *The Servant of the Lord and His Servant People*, Matthew S. Harmon
55 *Changed into His Likeness*, J. Gary Millar
56 *Piercing Leviathan*, Eric Ortlund
57 *Now and Not Yet*, Dean R. Ulrich
58 *The Glory of God and Paul*, Christopher W. Morgan and Robert A. Peterson
59 *From Prisoner to Prince*, Samuel Emadi
60 *The Royal Priest*, Matthew Emadi
61 *Life in the Son*, Clive Bowsher
62 *Answering the Psalmist's Perplexity*, James Hely Hutchinson
63 *'Egypt My People . . . and Israel My Inheritance'*, Daniel C. Timmer
64 *Impossible to be Restored?*, Marcus A. Mininger

An index of Scripture references for all the volumes may be found at http://www.thegospelcoalition.org/resources/nsbt.